Vernon Fuller

Volume II

THE REAL VOCAL BOOK

ISBN-13: 978-0-6340-6081-6
ISBN-10: 0-634-06081-3

7777 W. BLUEMOUND RD. P.O. BOX 13819 MILWAUKEE, WI 53213

For all works contained herein:
Unauthorized copying, arranging, adapting, recording or public performance is an infringement of copyright.
Infringers are liable under the law.

Visit Hal Leonard Online at
www.halleonard.com

PREFACE

The Real Vocal Book is the answer to the fake book. It is an alternative to the plethora of poorly designed, illegible, inaccurate, badly edited volumes which abound on the market today. The Real Vocal Book is extremely accurate, neat, and is designed, above all, for practical use. Every effort has been made to make it enjoyable to perform. Here are some of the primary features:

1. FORMAT
    a. The book is professionally copied and meticulously checked for accuracy in melody, harmony, and rhythms.
    b. Form within each song, including both phrases and larger sections, is clearly delineated and placed in obvious visual arrangement.
    c. All two-page songs open to face one another.
    d. Most standard-type songs remain true to their original harmonies with little or no reharmonization. The exceptions include a handful of jazz interpretations of popular songs and Broadway showtunes, as well as some modifications using modern notation and variation among turnarounds.

2. SELECTION OF TUNES AND EDITING
    a. Major jazz composers of the last 60 years are highlighted, with special attention given to the 1960s and 1970s.
    b. While some commonly played songs are absent from the book, many of the classics are here, including a fine selection of Duke Ellington masterpieces. Check out Real Vocal Book volume 1 for more songs.
    c. Many of the included arrangements represent the work of the jazz giants of the last 40 years.
    d. A number of songs by Rodgers & Hart/Hammerstein are included, as well as many songs by contemporary artists, including Sting, Norah Jones, Billy Joel and Lennon & McCartney.
    e. A variety of recordings and alternate editions were consulted to create the most accurate and user-friendly representations of these songs.

3. SOURCE REFERENCE
    a. The composer(s) of every tune is listed.
    b. Every song in the Real Vocal Book is now fully licensed for use.

THE REAL VOCAL BOOK

A

AC-CENT-TCHU-ATE THE POSITIVE	10
AFTER YOU'VE GONE	11
AIN'T MISBEHAVIN'	12
AIN'T THAT A KICK IN THE HEAD	13
ALL OR NOTHING AT ALL	14
ALL THE WAY	16
AREN'T YOU GLAD YOU'RE YOU	17
AS LONG AS I LIVE	18
AT SUNDOWN	19

B

BALI HA'I	20
BE CAREFUL, IT'S MY HEART	21
BEAT MY DOG	22
BEIN' GREEN	24
BÉSAME MUCHO (KISS ME MUCH)	26
THE BEST IS YET TO COME	28
THE BEST THING FOR YOU	29
THE BEST THINGS IN LIFE ARE FREE	30
BETWEEN THE DEVIL AND THE DEEP BLUE SEA	31
BEYOND THE BLUE HORIZON	32
BIG SPENDER	34
BLACK COFFEE	36
BLACKBIRD	38
A BLOSSOM FELL	33
BLUE ORCHIDS	40
THE BLUE ROOM	41
BORN TO BE BLUE	42
THE BREEZE AND I	43
BY MYSELF	44

C

CALDONIA (WHAT MAKES YOUR BIG HEAD SO HARD?)	46
CARAVAN	45
CHANGE PARTNERS	48
CHEEK TO CHEEK	50
CHICAGO (THAT TODDLIN' TOWN)	52
A COTTAGE FOR SALE	53
CRAZY	54
CRAZY HE CALLS ME	56
CRY ME A RIVER	57

D

DARN THAT DREAM	58
DAY DREAM	59
'DEED I DO	60
DON'T KNOW WHY	62
DON'T TAKE YOUR LOVE FROM ME	61
DON'T WORRY 'BOUT ME	64
DREAM A LITTLE DREAM OF ME	65
DREAM DANCING	66
A DREAMER'S HOLIDAY	68

E

EAST OF THE SUN (AND WEST OF THE MOON)	67
EASY STREET	70
THE END OF A LOVE AFFAIR	71
EV'RY TIME WE SAY GOODBYE	72
EVERYBODY LOVES MY BABY (BUT MY BABY DON'T LOVE NOBODY BUT ME)	73

EVERYBODY LOVES SOMEBODY 74
EVERYTHING HAPPENS TO ME 76
EXACTLY LIKE YOU 75

F

FALLING IN LOVE AGAIN
    (CAN'T HELP IT).........................78
FIELDS OF GOLD..79
FINE AND MELLOW......................................80
FOR EVERY MAN THERE'S A WOMAN......82
FROM HERE TO ETERNITY 83
FROM THIS MOMENT ON........................84

G

GLAD TO BE UNHAPPY............................86
THE GLORY OF LOVE 87
GOIN' OUT OF MY HEAD.........................88
GONE WITH THE WIND 89
A GOOD MAN IS HARD TO FIND 90
GOOD MORNING HEARTACHE 91
GOODBYE 92

H

HARD HEARTED HANNAH
    (THE VAMP OF SAVANNAH) 94
HAUNTED HEART 93
HEART AND SOUL....................................96
HEAT WAVE 97
HERE'S TO MY LADY 98
HEY, LOOK ME OVER 99
HOORAY FOR LOVE................................100
HOW ARE THINGS IN GLOCCA MORRA....102
HOW DEEP IS THE OCEAN
    (HOW HIGH IS THE SKY) 103

I

I AIN'T GOT NOBODY
    (AND NOBODY CARES FOR ME)....104
I AIN'T GOT NOTHIN' BUT THE BLUES....105
I CAN'T BELIEVE THAT
    YOU'RE IN LOVE WITH ME..........106
I CONCENTRATE ON YOU.......................108
I COULD HAVE DANCED ALL NIGHT 107
I CRIED FOR YOU 110
I DIDN'T KNOW WHAT TIME IT WAS 111
I DON'T KNOW ENOUGH ABOUT YOU 112
I DON'T KNOW WHY (I JUST DO) 113
I DON'T WANT TO WALK WITHOUT YOU....114
I GOT THE SUN IN THE MORNING 115
I GOTTA RIGHT TO SING THE BLUES......116
I GUESS I'LL HANG MY
    TEARS OUT TO DRY 117
I HEAR MUSIC 118
I KEEP GOING BACK TO JOE'S 119
I LEFT MY HEART IN SAN FRANCISCO....120
I LIKE THE LIKES OF YOU 121
1 WALK WITH MUSIC 122
I WANNA BE LOVED 123
I WISH I WERE IN LOVE AGAIN 124
I WISH YOU LOVE 125
I WISHED ON THE MOON 126
I WON'T DANCE 128
I'LL BE AROUND....................................127
I'LL BE SEEING YOU 130
I'LL GET BY (AS LONG AS I HAVE YOU)....131
I'LL TAKE ROMANCE 132
I'M ALWAYS CHASING RAINBOWS.........134
I'M GLAD THERE IS YOU (IN THIS WORLD
    OF ORDINARY PEOPLE) 135
I'M HIP...136

I'M OLD FASHIONED 138
I'VE GOT MY LOVE TO KEEP ME WARM....139
I'VE GOT THE WORLD ON A STRING 140
I'VE GOT YOU UNDER MY SKIN 142
I'VE GROWN ACCUSTOMED TO HER FACE....141
I'VE HEARD THAT SONG BEFORE 144
I'VE NEVER BEEN IN LOVE BEFORE 145
IF I DIDN'T CARE 146
ILL WIND (YOU'RE BLOWIN'
        ME NO GOOD) 147
IN LOVE IN VAIN 148
IN THE COOL, COOL,
        COOL OF THE EVENING 149
INDIAN SUMMER 150
IT ALL DEPENDS ON YOU 151
IT NEVER ENTERED MY MIND 152
IT ONLY HAPPENS WHEN
        I DANCE WITH YOU 153
IT'S A BIG WIDE WONDERFUL WORLD....154
IT'S A GOOD DAY 156
IT'S A LOVELY DAY TODAY 155
IT'S A MOST UNUSUAL DAY 158
IT'S BEEN A LONG, LONG TIME............160
IT'S DE-LOVELY 161
IT'S SO NICE TO HAVE
        A MAN AROUND THE HOUSE 162
IT'S THE TALK OF THE TOWN 163
IT'S TOO LATE 164
IT'S YOU OR NO ONE.............................166

J

JAVA JIVE 168
JUBILEE...167
JUST A GIGOLO.....................................170
JUST SQUEEZE ME
        (BUT DON'T TEASE ME).............171
JUST THE TWO OF US 172
JUST THE WAY YOU ARE 174

K

KILLING ME SOFTLY WITH HIS SONG 176

L

THE LADY IS A TRAMP 177
THE LADY'S IN LOVE WITH YOU............178
LAZYBONES 179
LEARNIN' THE BLUES............................180
LET THERE BE LOVE 181
LET THERE BE YOU 182
LET'S FACE THE MUSIC AND DANCE......184
LET'S GET AWAY FROM IT ALL..............183
LITTLE GIRL BLUE 186
LITTLE WHITE LIES 187
LOLLIPOPS AND ROSES 188
THE LOOK OF LOVE 189
LOOK TO THE RAINBOW 190
LOST IN THE STARS 192
L-O-V-E 191
LOVE IS A SIMPLE THING 194
LOVE LETTERS 195
LOVE ME OR LEAVE ME 196
LOVE YOU MADLY 197
LOVELY TO LOOK AT............................198
A LOVELY WAY TO SPEND AN EVENING....199
LOVER, COME BACK TO ME 200
LULLABY OF THE LEAVES 202

M

MAKIN' WHOOPEE!	203
THE MAN THAT GOT AWAY	204
MANHATTAN	206
MASQUERADE	207
(I'M AFRAID) THE MASQUERADE IS OVER	208
MEAN TO ME	209
MIDNIGHT SUN	210
MIMI	212
MONA LISA	213
MOONLIGHT BECOMES YOU	214
MOONLIGHT IN VERMONT	215
(THERE OUGHT TO BE A) MOONLIGHT SAVINGS TIME	216
MORE (TI GUARDERÒ NEL CUORE)	217
MORE I CANNOT WISH YOU	218
THE MOST BEAUTIFUL GIRL IN THE WORLD	220
MY ATTORNEY BERNIE	222
MY BABY JUST CARES FOR ME	224
MY BLUEBIRD	225
MY BLUE HEAVEN	226
MY BUDDY	227
MY HEART BELONGS TO DADDY	228
MY HEART STOOD STILL	229
MY IDEAL	230
MY LUCKY STAR	231
MY MAN (MON HOMME)	232
MY MELANCHOLY BABY	234
MY SHIP	236
MY SILENT LOVE	237
MY SIN	238

N

NANCY - WITH THE LAUGHING FACE	239
NEVER LET ME GO	240
NEVERTHELESS (I'M IN LOVE WITH YOU)	241
A NIGHTINGALE SANG IN BERKELEY SQUARE	242
NO MOON AT ALL	243
NOBODY ELSE BUT ME	244
NORWEGIAN WOOD (THIS BIRD HAS FLOWN)	245

O

OL' MAN RIVER	246
OLD CAPE COD	247
ON A CLEAR DAY (YOU CAN SEE FOREVER)	248
ON A SLOW BOAT TO CHINA	249
ON THE SOUTH SIDE OF CHICAGO	250
ON THE STREET WHERE YOU LIVE	252
ON THE SUNNY SIDE OF THE STREET	251
ONE FOR MY BABY (AND ONE MORE FOR THE ROAD)	254

P

THE PARTY'S OVER	256
PEEL ME A GRAPE	258
PENTHOUSE SERENADE	257
PEOPLE	260
POINCIANA (SONG OF THE TREE)	262
POOR BUTTERFLY	264
PRELUDE TO A KISS	265
PRETEND	266
PURE IMAGINATION	267
PUT ON A HAPPY FACE	268

Q

QUIZÁS, QUIZÁS, QUIZÁS (PERHAPS,
    PERHAPS, PERHAPS) 270

R

THE RAINBOW CONNECTION 269
RIDIN' HIGH 272
ROBERT FROST 274
ROCKIN' CHAIR 273

S

SAME OLD SATURDAY NIGHT 276
SAY IT ISN'T SO 277
SAY IT WITH MUSIC 278
SCOTCH AND SODA 279
SEEMS LIKE OLD TIMES 280
SENTIMENTAL ME 281
SHINE 282
SHOO FLY PIE AND APPLE PAN DOWDY 283
SING, YOU SINNERS 284
SKYLARK 285
SKYLINER 286
SLEEP WARM 287
A SLEEPIN' BEE 288
SMALL FRY 290
SMALL WORLD 289
SO IN LOVE 292
SOFT LIGHTS AND SWEET MUSIC 294
SOMEBODY LOVES YOU 295
SOMETHING WONDERFUL 296
SOMETIMES I'M HAPPY 297
THE SONG IS ENDED (BUT THE
    MELODY LINGERS ON) 298
SOON IT'S GONNA RAIN 299
SPEAK LOW 300
SPRING CAN REALLY
    HANG YOU UP THE MOST 302
SPRING WILL BE A LITTLE
    LATE THIS YEAR 304
ST. LOUIS BLUES 305
STEPPIN' OUT WITH MY BABY 306
STORMY WEATHER (KEEPS RAININ'
    ALL THE TIME) 307
STRANGERS IN THE NIGHT 308
SWAY (QUIEN SERA) 309
SWEET AND LOVELY 310
SWINGING ON A STAR 311

T

TALK TO ME 312
A TASTE OF HONEY 313
TEACH ME TONIGHT 314
TELEPHONE SONG 315
TEN CENTS A DANCE 316
(LOVE IS) THE TENDER TRAP 318
THAT OLD BLACK MAGIC 320
THAT OLD FEELING 317
THAT'S LIFE 322
THERE ARE SUCH THINGS 323
THERE'S NO YOU 324
THEY SAY IT'S WONDERFUL 325
THINGS AIN'T WHAT THEY USED TO BE 326
THIS CAN'T BE LOVE 327
THIS COULD BE THE
    START OF SOMETHING BIG 328
THIS IS ALL I ASK (BEAUTIFUL GIRLS
    WALK A LITTLE SLOWER) 330
THIS LOVE OF MINE 331
THREE LITTLE WORDS 332
TIME AFTER TIME 333
TO LOVE AND BE LOVED 334
TOO CLOSE FOR COMFORT 335
TOO LATE NOW 336
THE TOUCH OF YOUR LIPS 337
TWO SLEEPY PEOPLE 338

U

UNFORGETTABLE 339

V

THE VERY THOUGHT OF YOU 340
VIOLETS FOR YOUR FURS 341

W

WALKIN' MY BABY BACK HOME 342
WALTZ FOR DEBBY................................344
WHAT A DIFF'RENCE A DAY MADE 343
WHAT A WONDERFUL WORLD...............346
WHAT I DID FOR LOVE 348
WHAT NOW MY LOVE 350
WHERE OR WHEN.................................349
WHY DON'T YOU DO RIGHT
    (GET ME SOME MONEY, TOO!) 352
WILL YOU STILL BE MINE.....................354
WITCHCRAFT 356
WITH EVERY BREATH I TAKE................357
WOULDN'T IT BE LOVERLY 358
WRAP YOUR TROUBLES IN DREAMS (AND
    DREAM YOUR TROUBLES AWAY)....359

Y

YOU ARE BEAUTIFUL 360
YOU BELONG TO MY HEART
    (SOLAMENTE UNA VEZ).............361
YOU BETTER GO NOW 362
YOU CAN DEPEND ON ME.....................363
YOU MADE ME LOVE YOU
    (I DIDN'T WANT TO DO IT) 364
YOU'RE DRIVING ME CRAZY!
    (WHAT DID I DO?) 365
YOU'RE MY EVERYTHING 366
YOUNGER THAN SPRINGTIME...............367

Aren't You Glad You're You

(Med.)

Jimmy Van Heusen / Johnny Burke

Ev-'ry time you're near a rose, aren't you glad you've got a nose?
And if the dawn is fresh with dew, aren't you glad you're you?
When a mead-ow-lark ap-pears, aren't you glad you've got two ears?
And if your heart is sing-ing, too, aren't you glad you're you? You can
see a sum-mer sky or touch a friend-ly hand or
taste an ap-ple pie. Par-don the gram-mar, but ain't life grand?
And when you wake up each morn, aren't you glad that you were born?
Think what you've got the whole day through, aren't you glad you're you?

Copyright © 1945 by Bourne Co. and Dorsey Bros. Music, A Division of Music Sales Corporation
Copyright Renewed

(MED.)

AT SUNDOWN

—WALTER DONALDSON

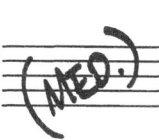

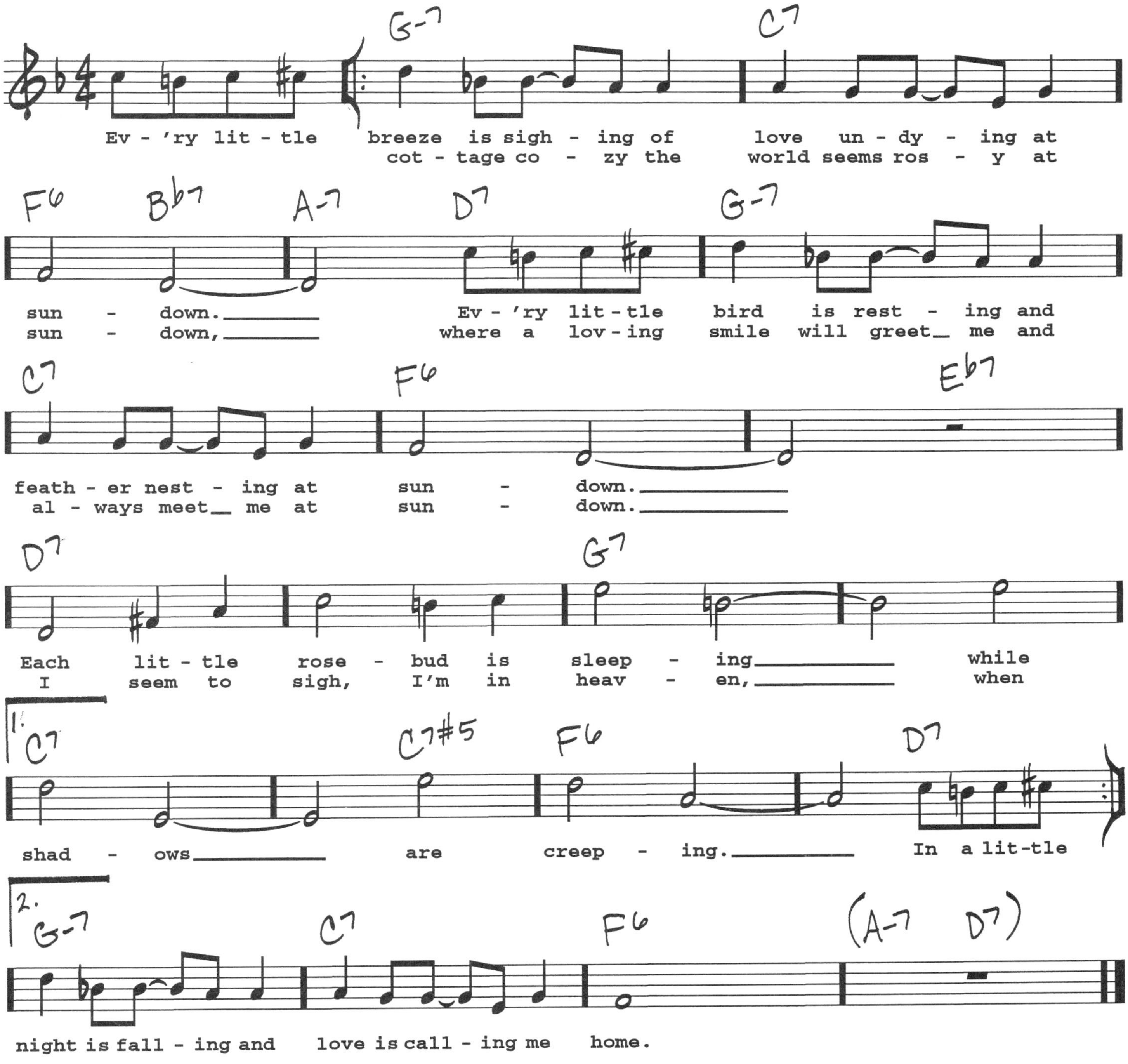

(MED.)

BE CAREFUL, IT'S MY HEART

-IRVING BERLIN

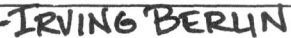

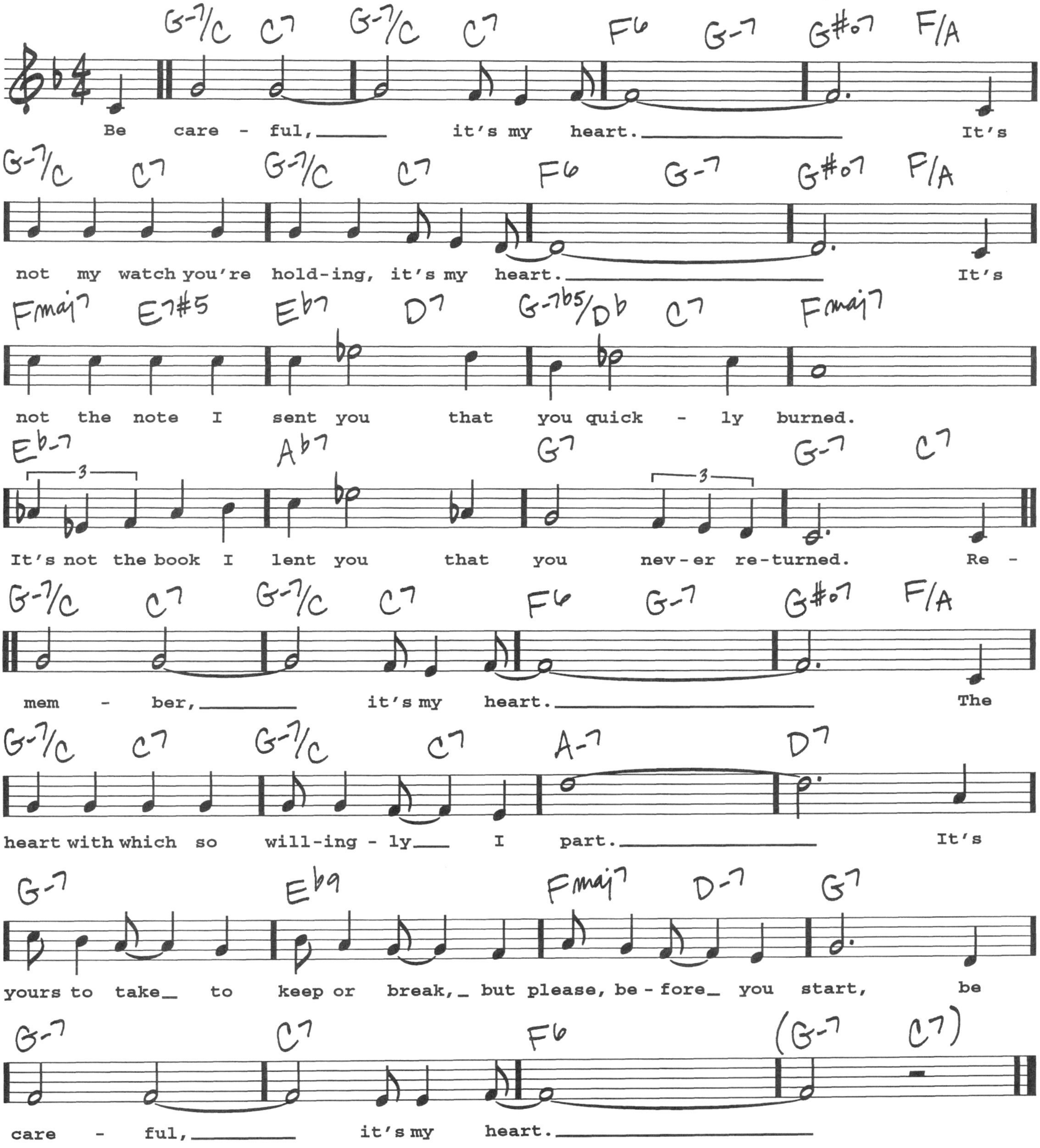

(SLOW BLUES)

BLACK COFFEE

–PAUL FRANCIS WEBSTER/
SONNY BURKE

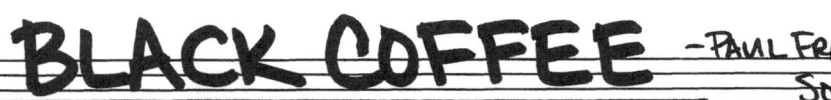

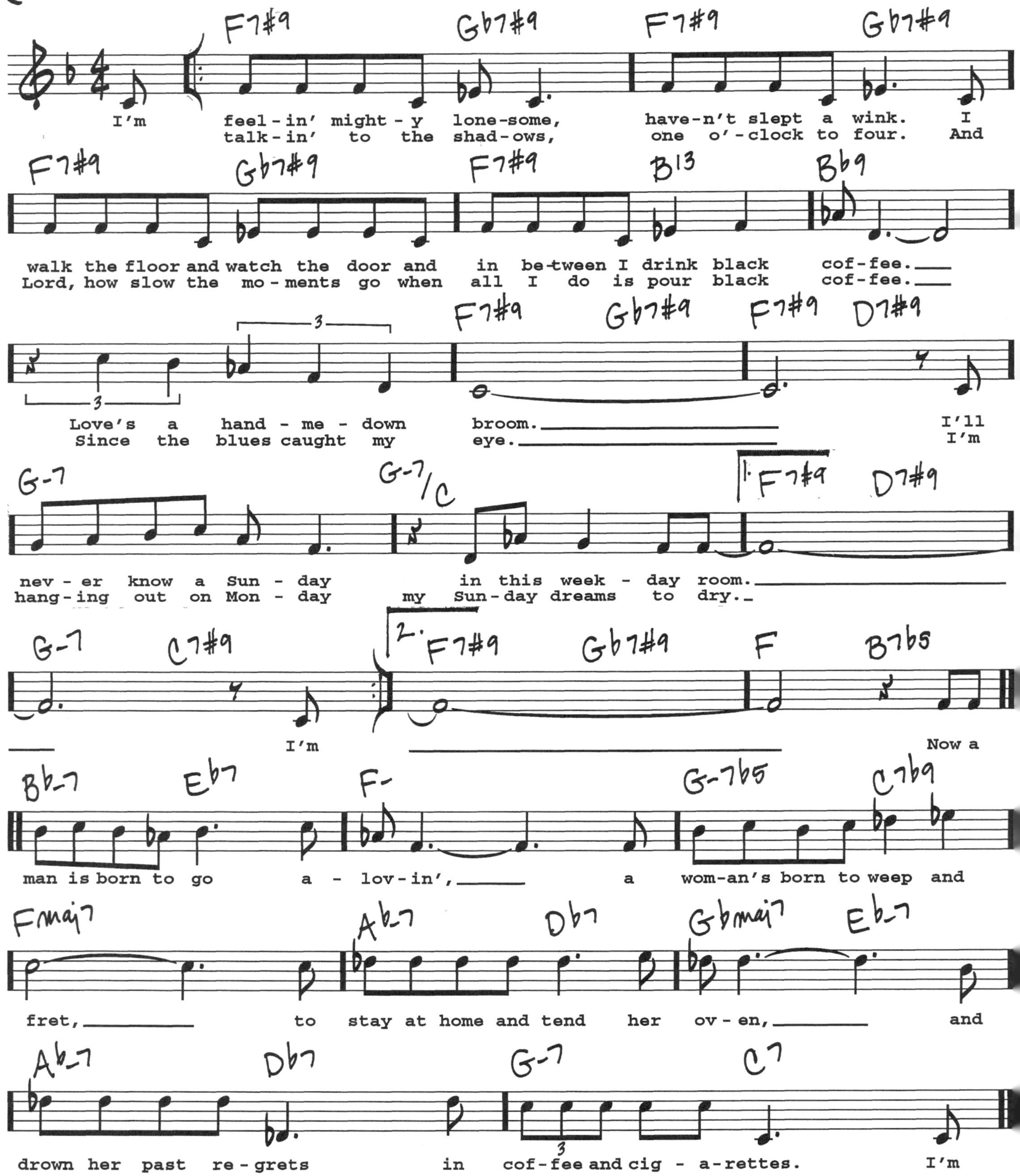

BLACKBIRD

(SLOW)

-JOHN LENNON/
PAUL McCARTNEY

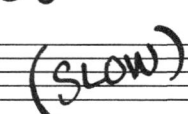

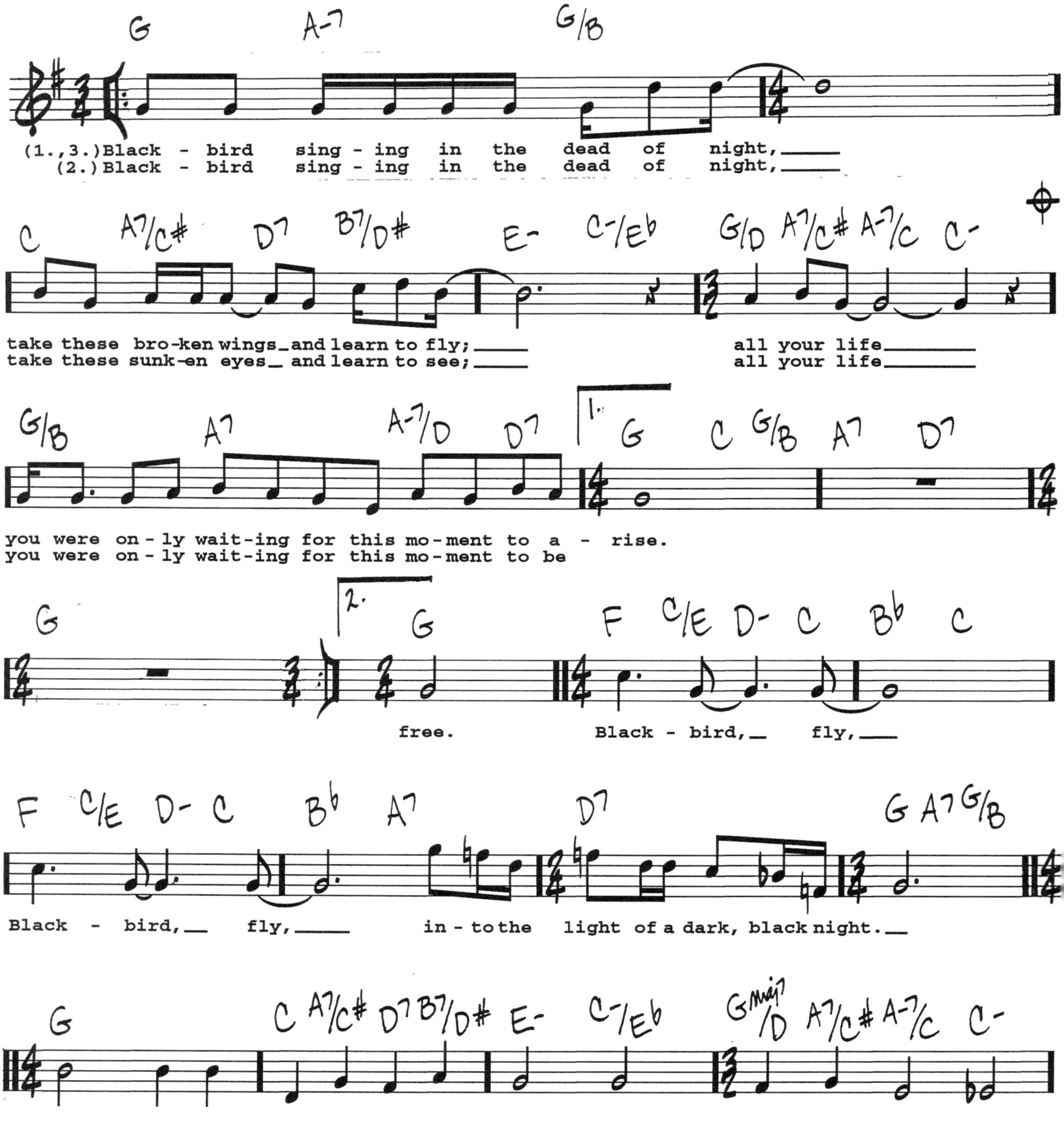

(MED.)

THE BLUE ROOM

– RICHARD RODGERS/
LORENZ HART

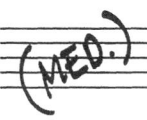

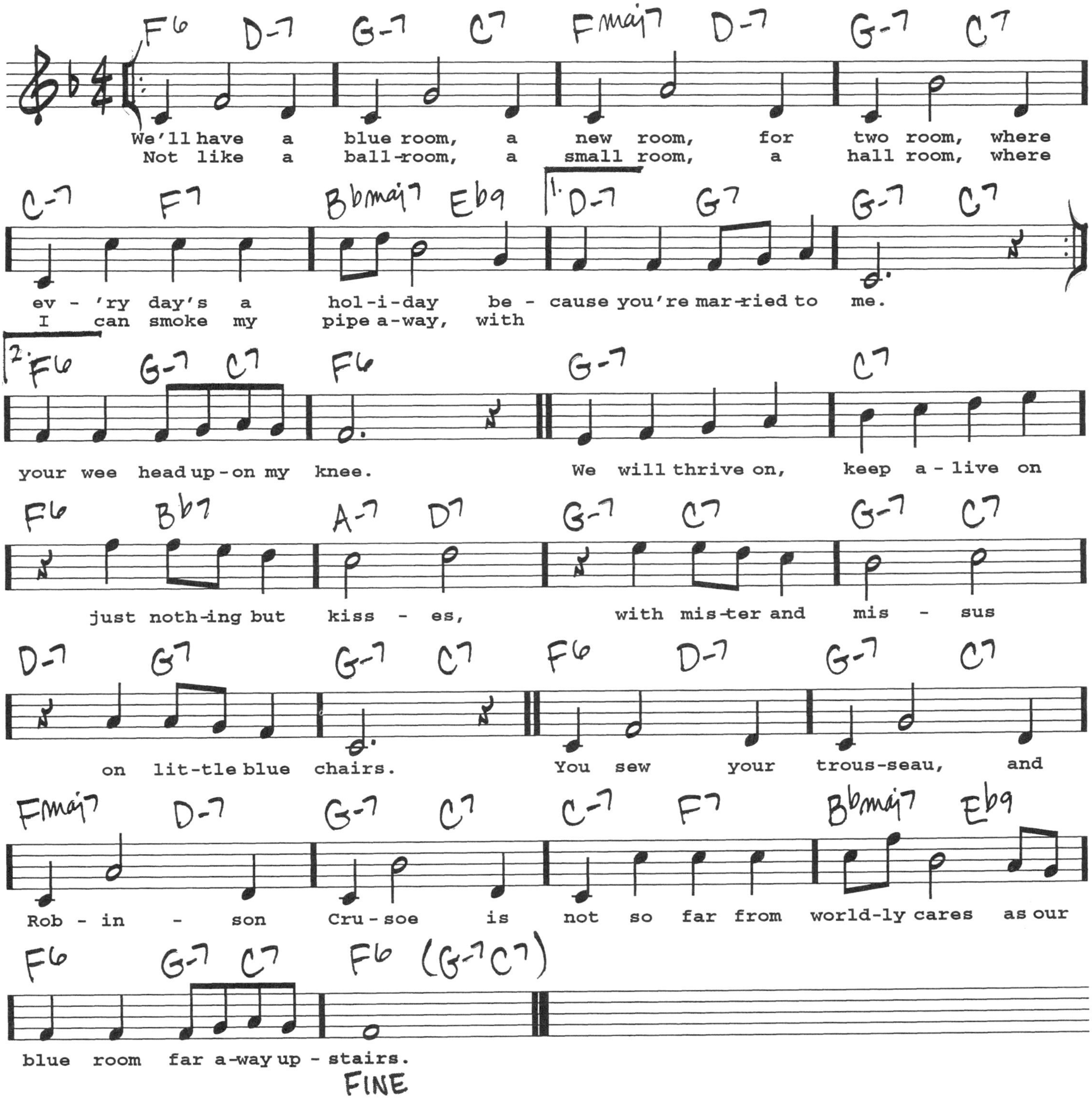

(RHUMBA)

THE BREEZE AND I

- ERNESTO LECUONA/
AL STILLMAN

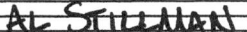

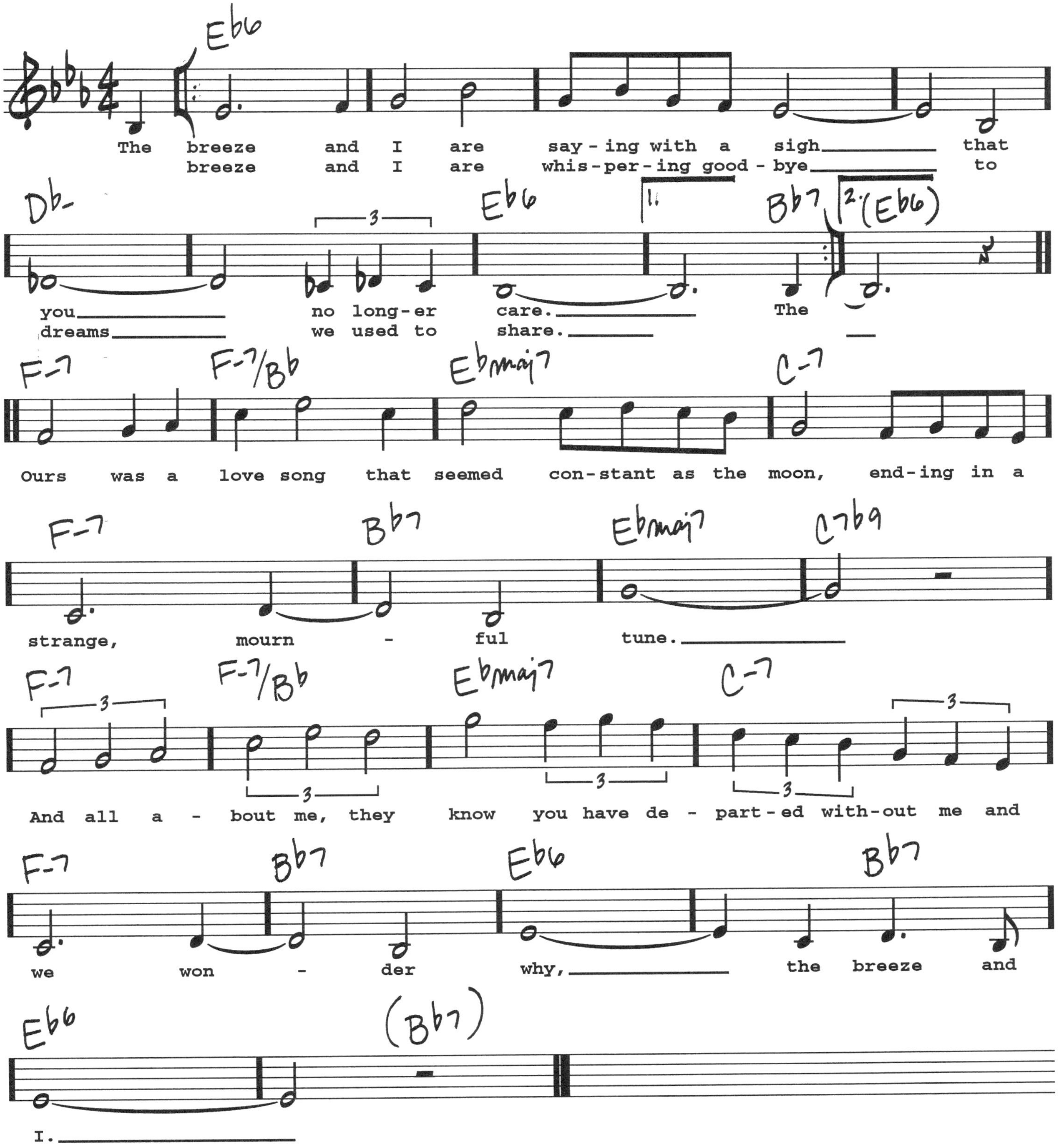

(MED. BALLAD)

DARN THAT DREAM

-JIMMY VAN HEUSEN/
EDDIE DE LANGE

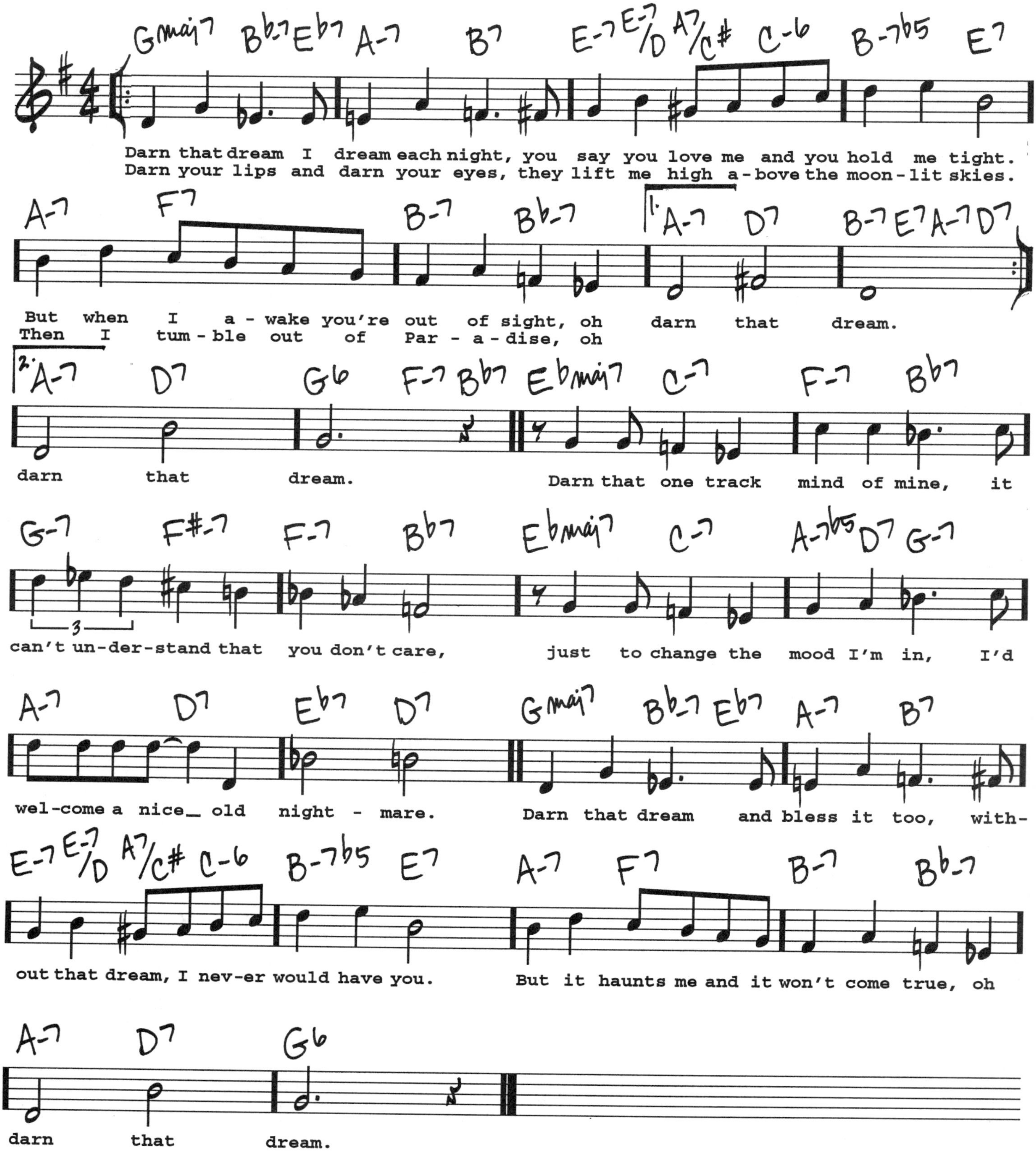

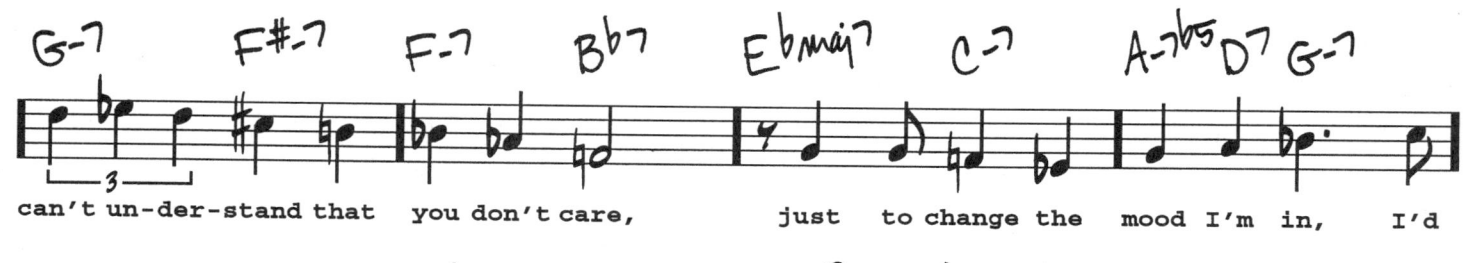

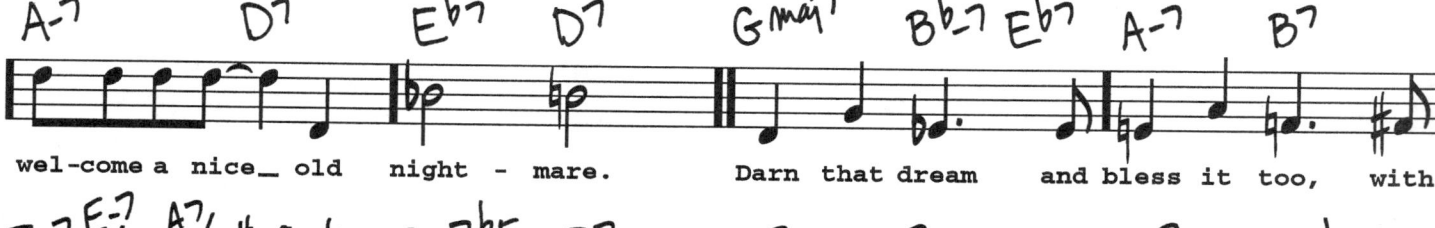

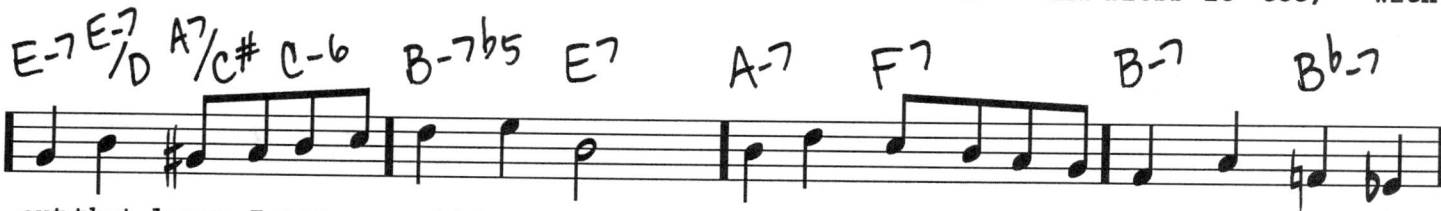

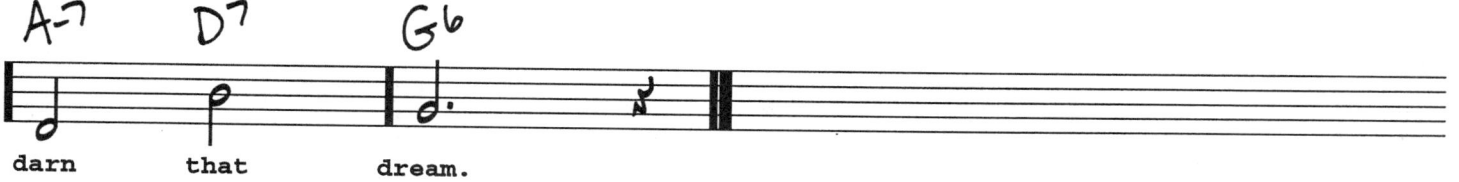

Dream Dancing
— Cole Porter

(Med. or Bossa)

Verse 1:
When day is gone and night comes on, 'til the dawn what do I do? I clasp your hand and wander through slumberland, dream dancing with you.

Verse 2:
Dance between a night sky serene and fields of green, sparkling with dew. It's joy sublime, whenever I spend my time dream dancing with you.

We dream dancing, oh, what a lucky windfall! Touching you, clutching you all the night through. So say you love me dear, and let me make my career dream dancing, to paradise prancing, dream dancing with you.

Chords (in order of appearance):
E7#5 | Amaj7 | D-7 | G7 | Cmaj7 | Gb7b5 | Fmaj7 | Bb9 | Cmaj7 | F7(#11) | E-7 | A7 | Eb-7 | Ab7 | D-7 | G7 | Cmaj7 | G-7 | C7 | Fmaj7 | Bb9 | Cmaj7 | G7 | C6 | D7 | A-7b5 | D7b9 | D-7 | G7sus4 | Cmaj7 | Gb7b5 | Fmaj7(#11) | E-7 | A7 | Eb-7 | Ab7 | D-7 | G7 | Eb-7 | Ab7 | D-7 | G7 | Eb-7 | Ab7 | D-7 | G7sus4 | C6

Copyright © 1941 by Chappell & Co.
Copyright Renewed, Assigned to John F. Wharton, Trustee of the Cole Porter Musical and Literary Property Trusts
Chappell & Co. owner of publication and allied rights throughout the world

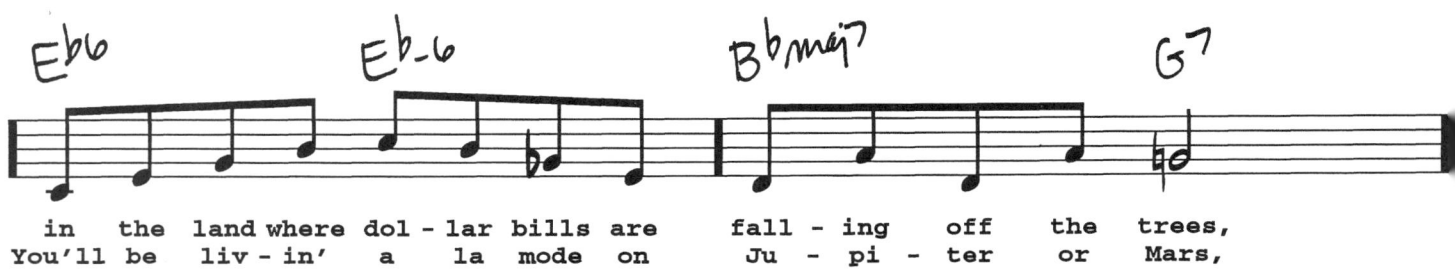

Ev'ry Time We Say Goodbye

(Ballad) — Cole Porter

(BALLAD)

EVERYTHING HAPPENS TO ME

-MATT DENNIS/TOM ADAIR

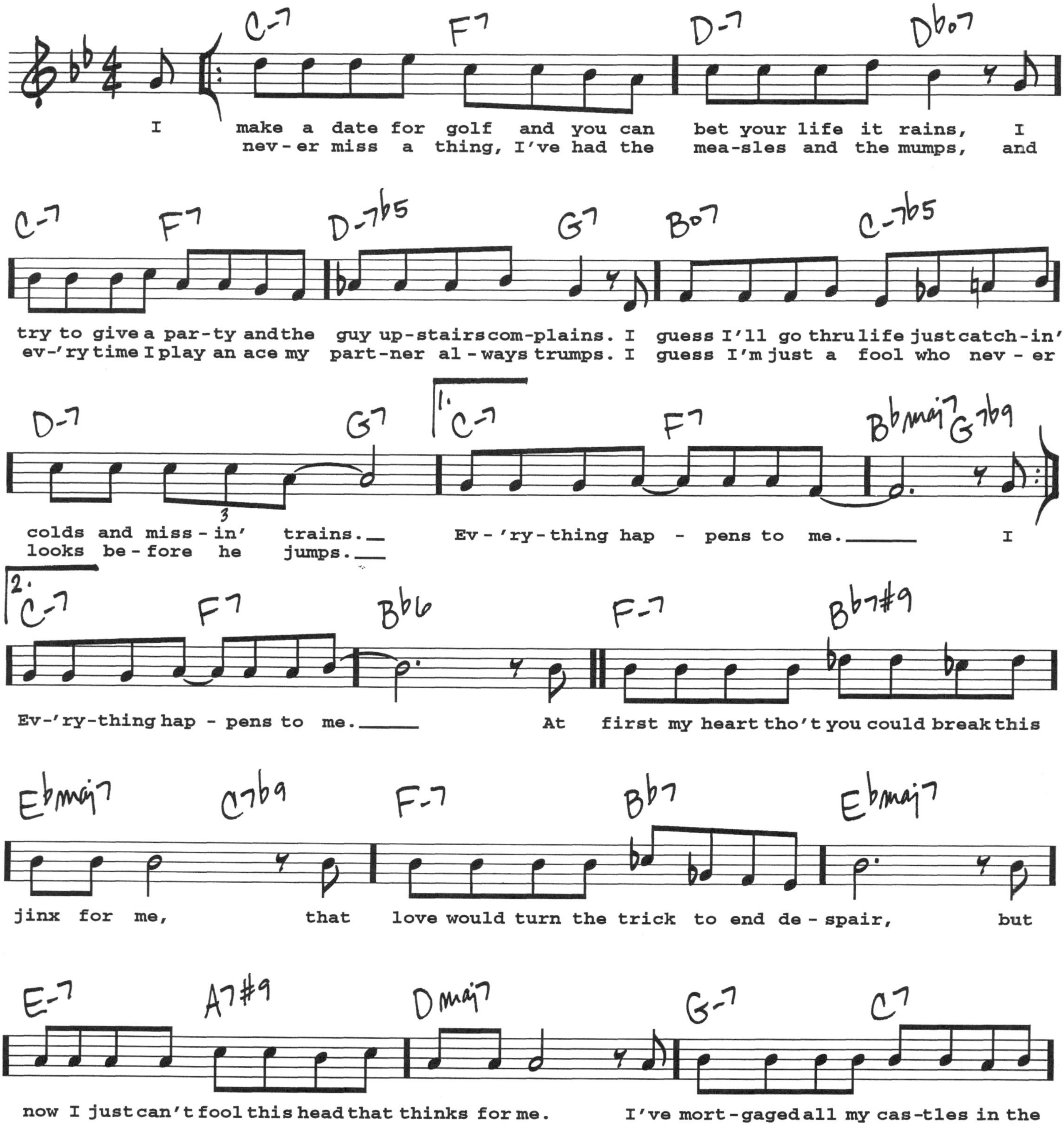

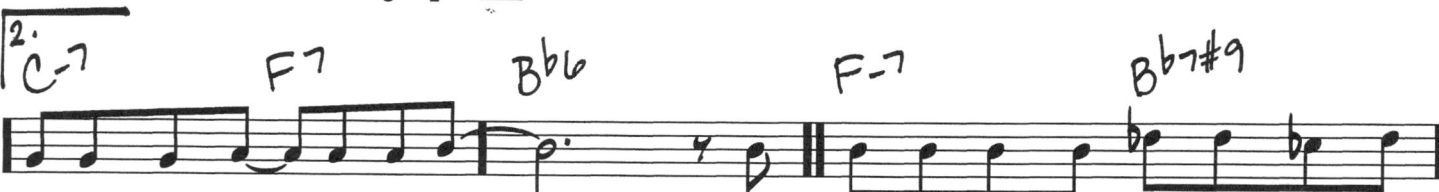

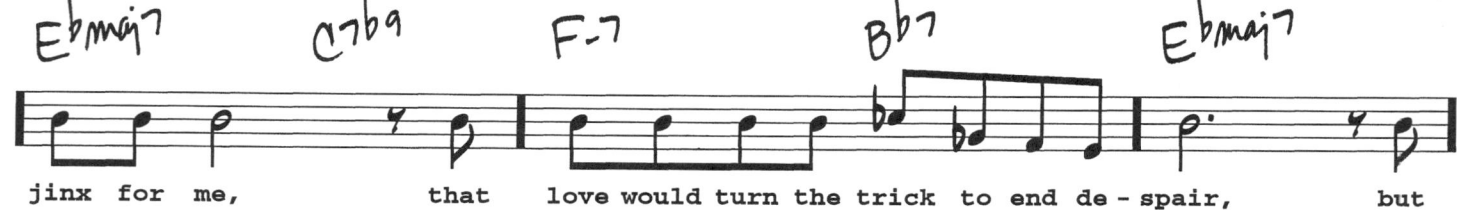

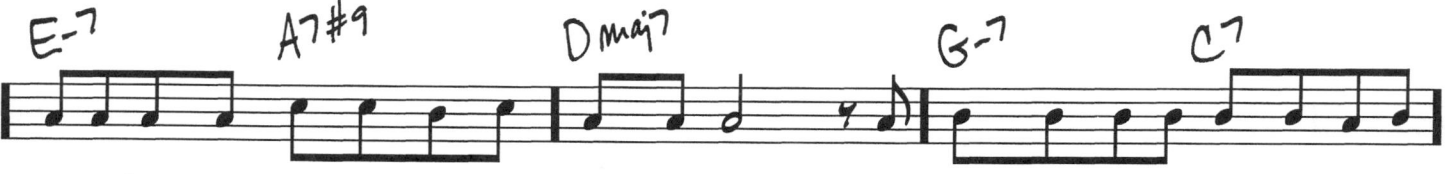

FIELDS OF GOLD

— STING

(MED. EVEN 8ths)

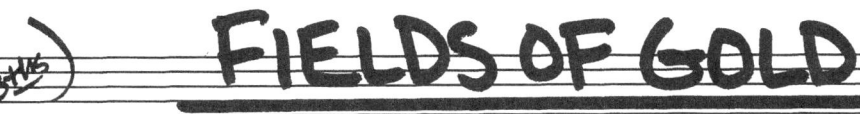

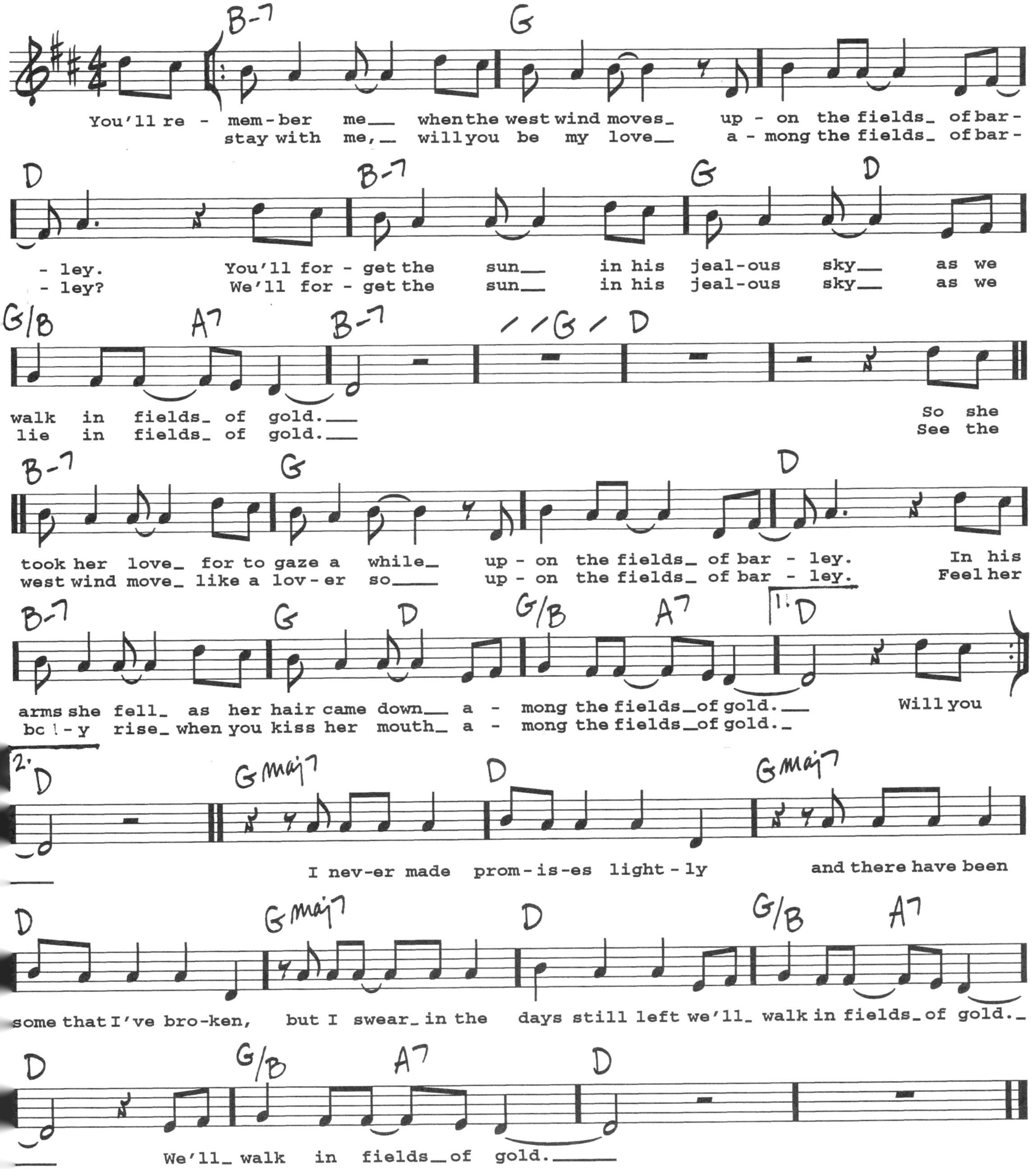

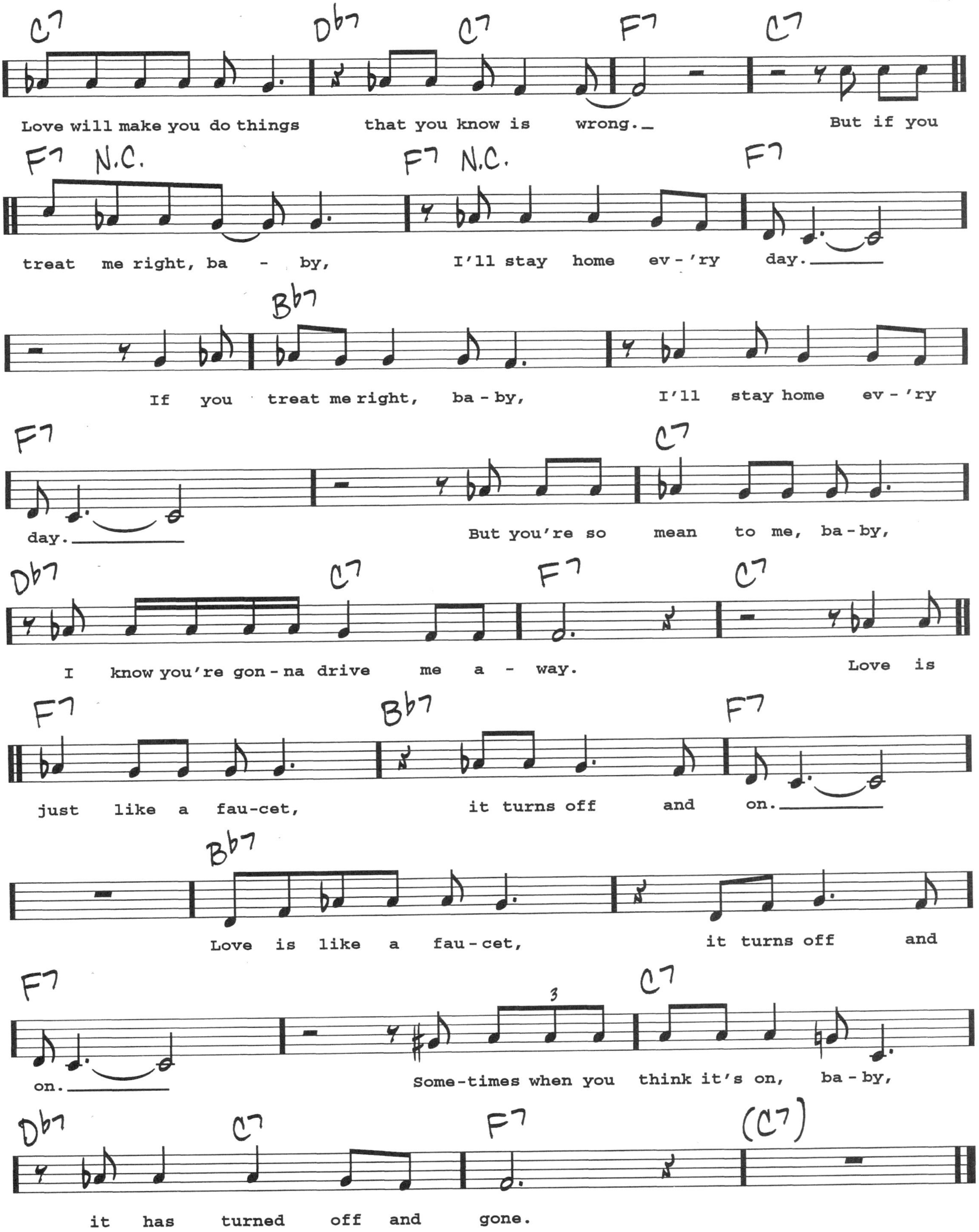
C7 D♭7 C7 F7 C7
Love will make you do things that you know is wrong._ But if you
F7 N.C. F7 N.C. F7
treat me right, ba - by, I'll stay home ev - 'ry day.
B♭7
If you treat me right, ba - by, I'll stay home ev - 'ry
F7 C7
day. But you're so mean to me, ba - by,
D♭7 C7 F7 C7
I know you're gon - na drive me a - way. Love is
F7 B♭7 F7
just like a fau - cet, it turns off and on.
B♭7
Love is like a fau - cet, it turns off and
F7 C7
on. Some - times when you think it's on, ba - by,
D♭7 C7 F7 (C7)
it has turned off and gone.

(BALLAD)

GOOD MORNING HEARTACHE

-DAN FISHER/IRENE HIGGINBOTHAM/ERVIN DRAKE

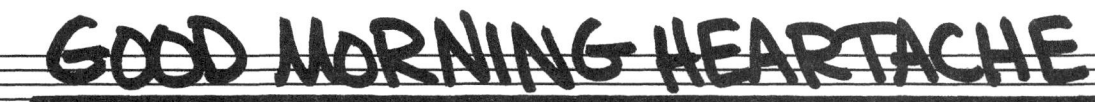

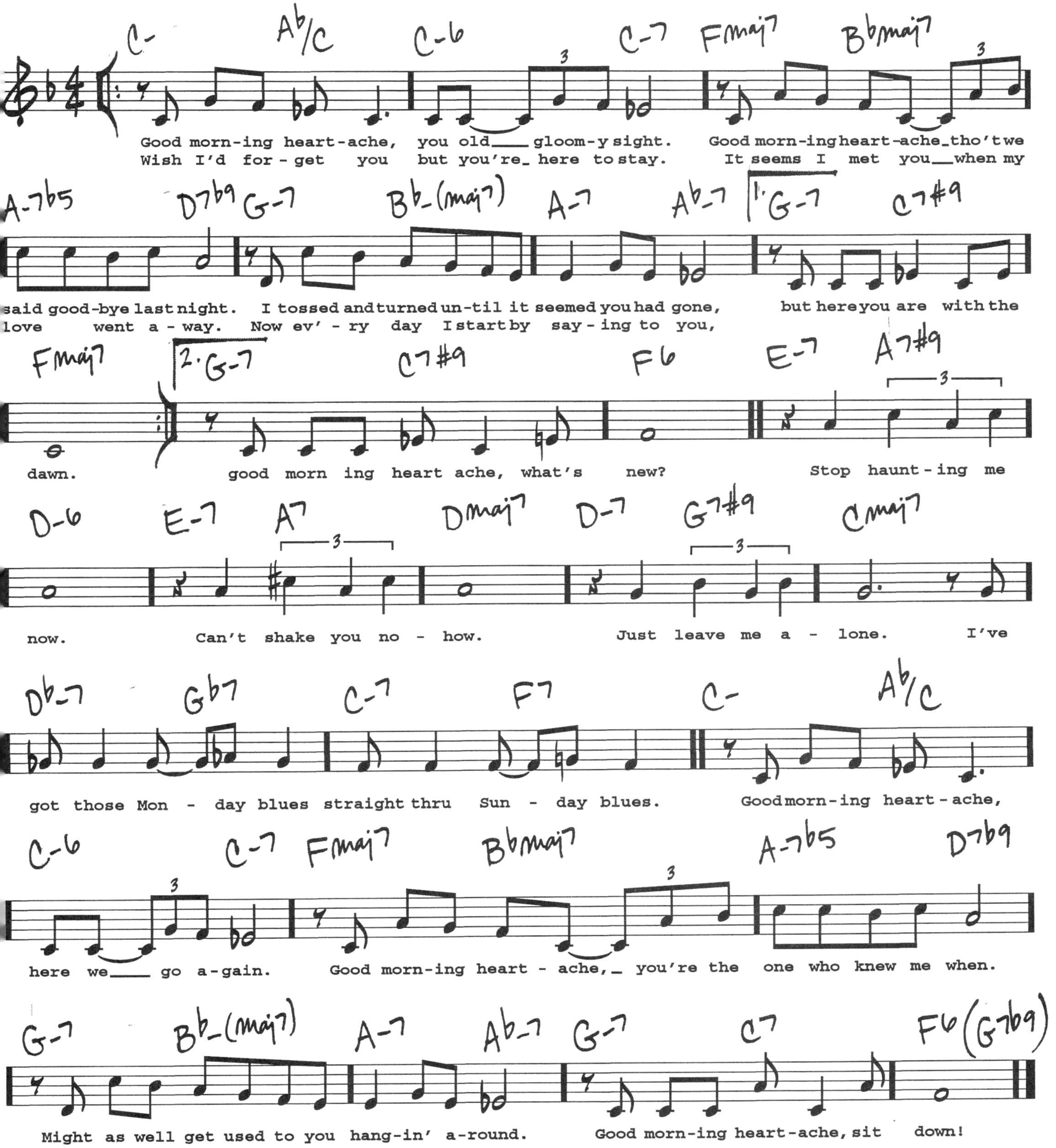

I Ain't Got Nobody (And Nobody Cares For Me)

—Spencer Williams / Dave Peyton / Roger Graham

(Med. Swing)

I_____ ain't got no-bod-y, and_____ no-bod-y cares for me.

And_____ I'm sad and lone-ly, won't some-bod-y come and take a chance with me?_____

I'll sing sweet love songs, hon-ey, all the time,_____ if you'll come and be my sweet ba-by mine._____ 'Cause

I_____ ain't got no-bod-y, and_____ no-bod-y cares for me.

I Don't Know Enough About You

— Peggy Lee / Dave Barbour

(Med.)

I know a little bit about a lot of things, but
I don't know enough about you.
Just when I think you're mine you try a
diff'rent line, and, baby, what can I do?
I read the latest news, no buttons on my shoes, but,
baby, I'm confused about you.
You get me in a spin; oh, what a stew I'm in,
'cause I don't know enough about you.

Jack of all trades, master of none
and isn't it a shame?
I'm so sure that you'd be good for me
if you'd only play my game.
You know I went to school and I'm nobody's fool,
that is to say, until I met you.
I know a little bit about a lot of things, but
I don't know enough about you.

(BALLAD) I DON'T KNOW WHY (I JUST DO)

-FRED E. AHLERT/ROY TURK

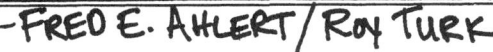

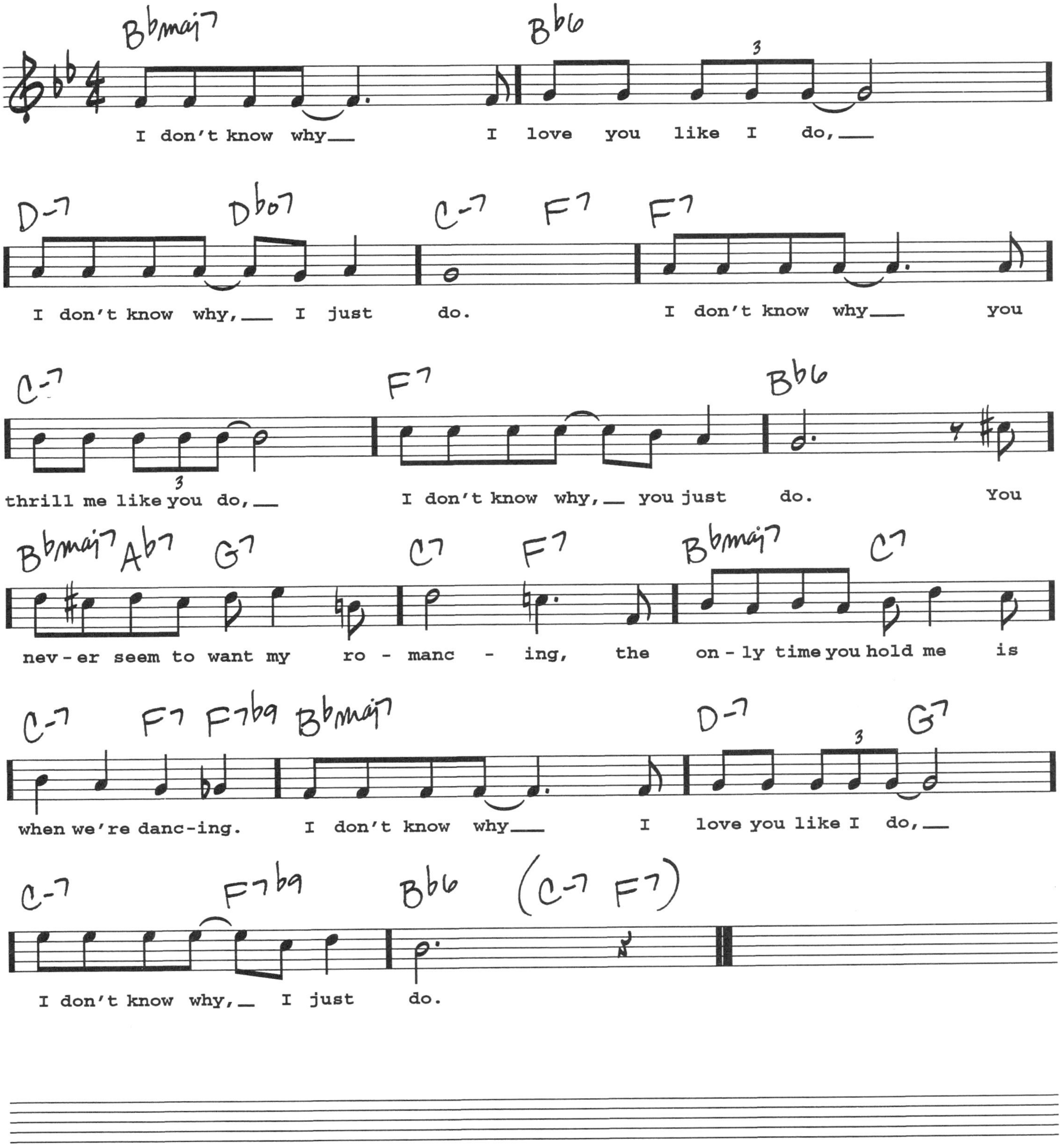

I Wish I Were In Love Again

— Richard Rodgers / Lorenz Hart

(Med.)

124

The sleep-less nights, the dai-ly fights, the quick to-bog-gan when you reach the heights; I miss the kiss-es and I miss the bites. I wish I were in love a-gain!

The bro-ken dates, the end-less waits, the love-ly lov-ing and the hate-ful hates, the con-ver-sa-tion with the fly-ing plates; I wish I were in love a-gain!

No more pain, no more strain. Now I'm sane, but I would rath-er be ga-ga! The pulled-out fur of cat and cur, the fine mis-mat-ing of a him and her; I've learned my les-son, but I wish I were in love a-gain!

Copyright © 1937 (Renewed) by Chappell & Co.
Rights for the Extended Renewal Term in the U.S. Controlled by Williamson Music and WB Music Corp.
o/b/o The Estate Of Lorenz Hart

I've Never Been In Love Before

- Frank Loesser

(Ballad)

I've nev-er been in love be-fore; now all at once it's you. It's you for-ev-er-more. I've

nev-er been in love be-fore; I thought my heart was safe, I thought I knew the score. But this is wine that's all too strange and strong, I'm full of fool-ish song and out my song must pour. So please for-give this help-less haze I'm in, I've real-ly nev-er been in love be-fore.

© 1950 (Renewed) FRANK MUSIC CORP.

It's A Big Wide Wonderful World

154
(MED. WALTZ)

– John Rox

It's a big wide won-der-ful world you live in.
brave new star-span-gled sky a-bove you.

When you're in love, you're a mas-ter of all you sur-vey; you're a gay San-ta Claus.
When you're in love, you're a he-ro, a Ne-ro, A-pol-lo, the Wiz-ard of Oz.

There's a
You've a king-dom, pow-er and glo-ry, the old, old, old-est of sto-ries is new, true. You've built your Rome in just one day. Life is mys-tic, a mid-sum-mer's night, you live in, a Turk-ish De-light, you're in heav-en. It's swell when you're real-ly in love.

© 1939, 1940 Gower Music, Inc.
© Renewed EDWIN H. MORRIS & COMPANY, A Division of MPL Music Publishing, Inc.

Look to the Rainbow

(Ballad)

— Burton Lane / E.Y. "Yip" Harburg

190

On the day I was born, said my father, said he, I've an el-e-gant leg-a-cy wait-in' for ye. 'Tis a rhyme for your lips and a song for your heart, to sing it when-ev-er the world falls a-part.

Sump-tu-ous gift to be-queath to a child, oh the lure of that song kept her feet run-nin' wild. For you nev-er grow old and you nev-er stood still, with whip-poor-wills sing-in' be-yond the next hill.

Look, look, look to the rain-bow, fol-low it o-ver the hill and stream. Look, look, look to the rain-bow, fol-low the fel-low who fol-lows a dream. 'Twas a dream. Fol-low the fel-low, fol-low the fel-low, fol-low the fel-low who fol-lows a dream.

SOLOS – TAKE 1ST ENDING ONLY

Copyright © 1946, 1947 by Chappell & Co. and Glocca Morra Music
Copyright Renewed
All Rights for Glocca Morra Music Administered by Next Decade Entertainment, Inc.

MAKIN' WHOOPEE!

- WALTER DONALDSON/ GUS KAHN

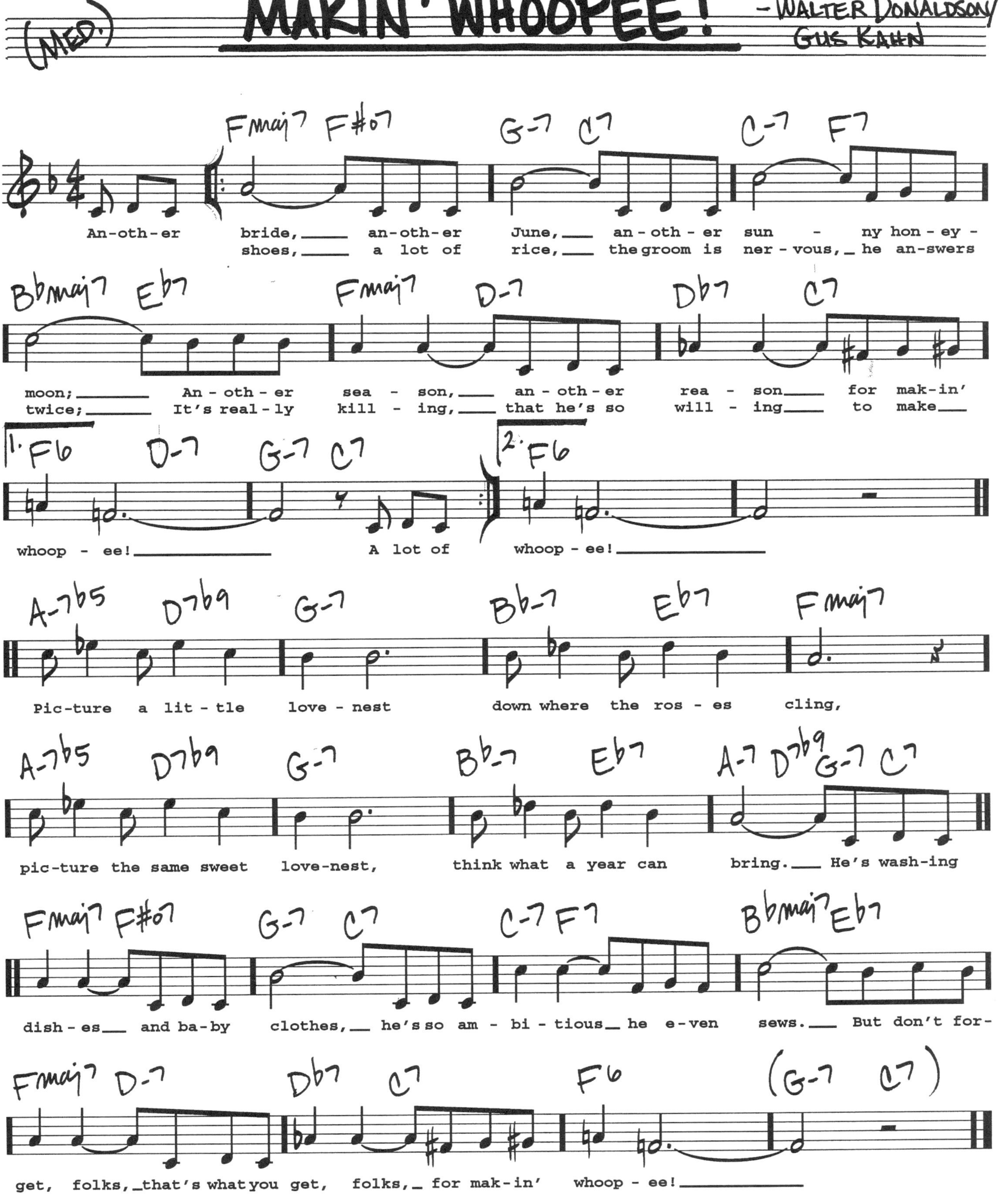

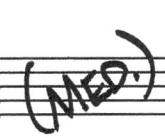

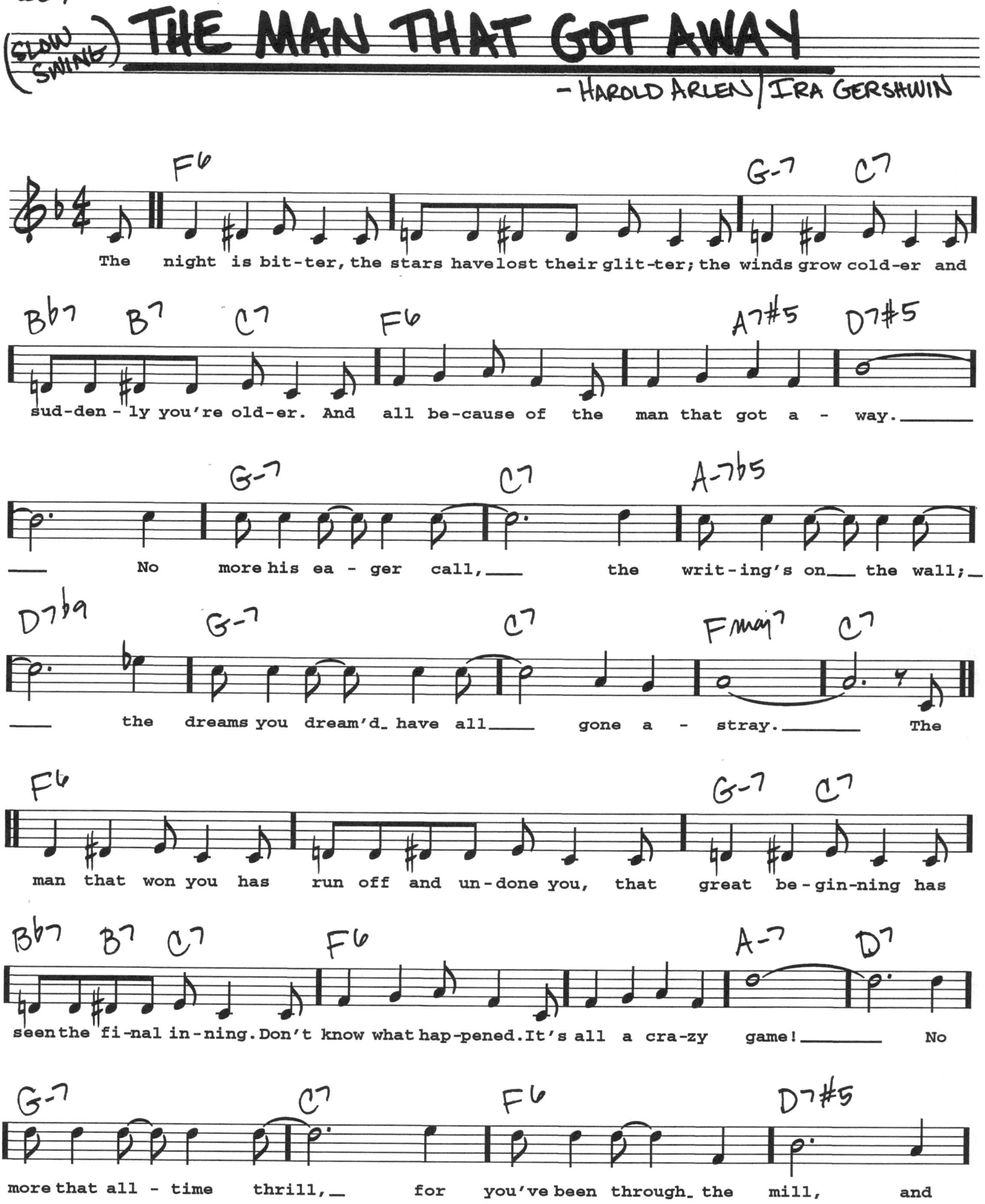
(SLOW SWING)
THE MAN THAT GOT AWAY
- HAROLD ARLEN / IRA GERSHWIN
The night is bit-ter, the stars have lost their glit-ter; the winds grow cold-er and
sud-den - ly you're old-er. And all be-cause of the man that got a - way.
No more his ea - ger call, the writ-ing's on the wall;
the dreams you dream'd have all gone a - stray. The
man that won you has run off and un-done you, that great be-gin-ning has
seen the fi-nal in-ning. Don't know what hap-pened. It's all a cra-zy game! No
more that all - time thrill, for you've been through the mill, and

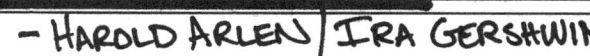

MONA LISA

(BALLAD)

–JAY LIVINGSTON/
RAY EVANS

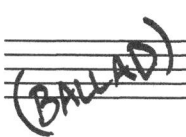

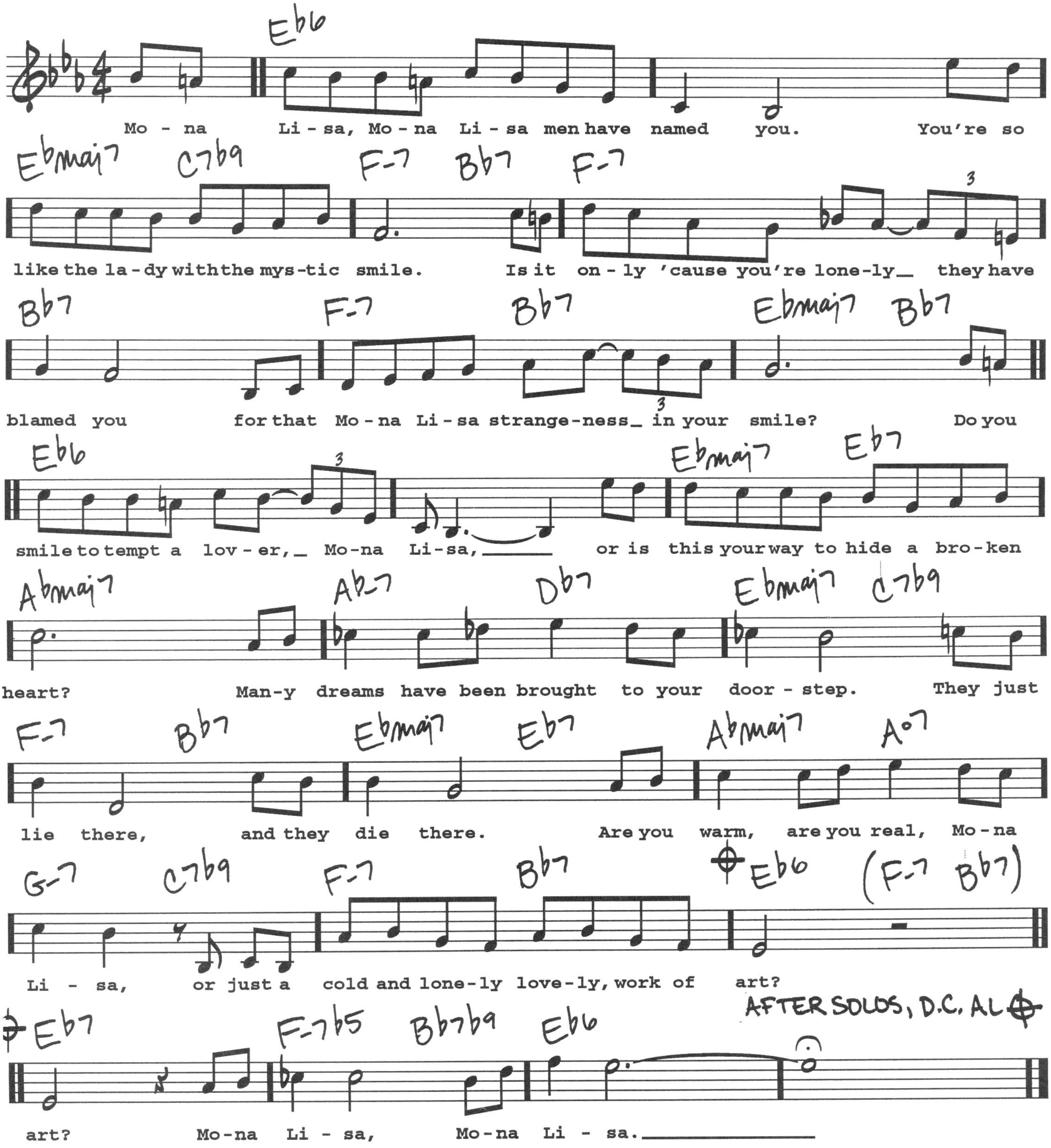

MORE
(TI GUARDERÒ NEL CUORE)

(MED. LATIN)

–NINO OLIVIERO/ RIZ ORTOLANI/ MARCELLO CIORCIOLINI/NORMAN NEWELL

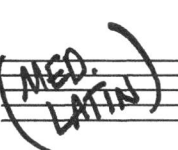

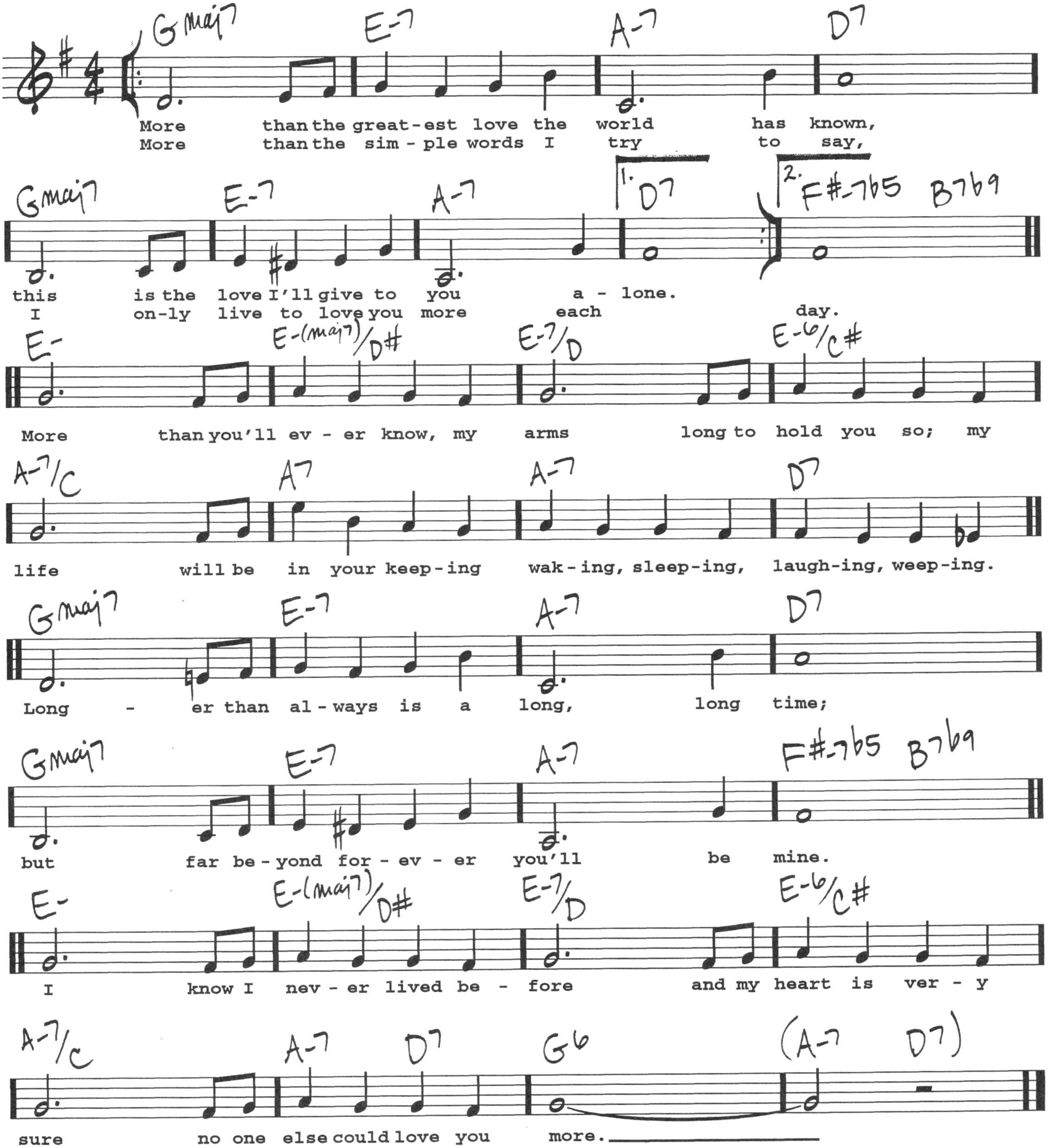

(BALLAD)
MY BUDDY
-WALTER DONALDSON/
GUS KAHN
Gmaj7 G#o7 A-7 D7
Nights are long since you went a - way. I
Miss your voice, the touch of your hand, just
G6 Bbo7 A-7 D7
think a - bout you all through the day, my
long to know that you un - der - stand, my
G6 G7/F E7
bud - dy, my bud - dy, no
bud - dy, my bud - dy, your
A-7 1. A7 A-7 D7
bud - dy quite so true.
2. D7 G6
miss - es you.

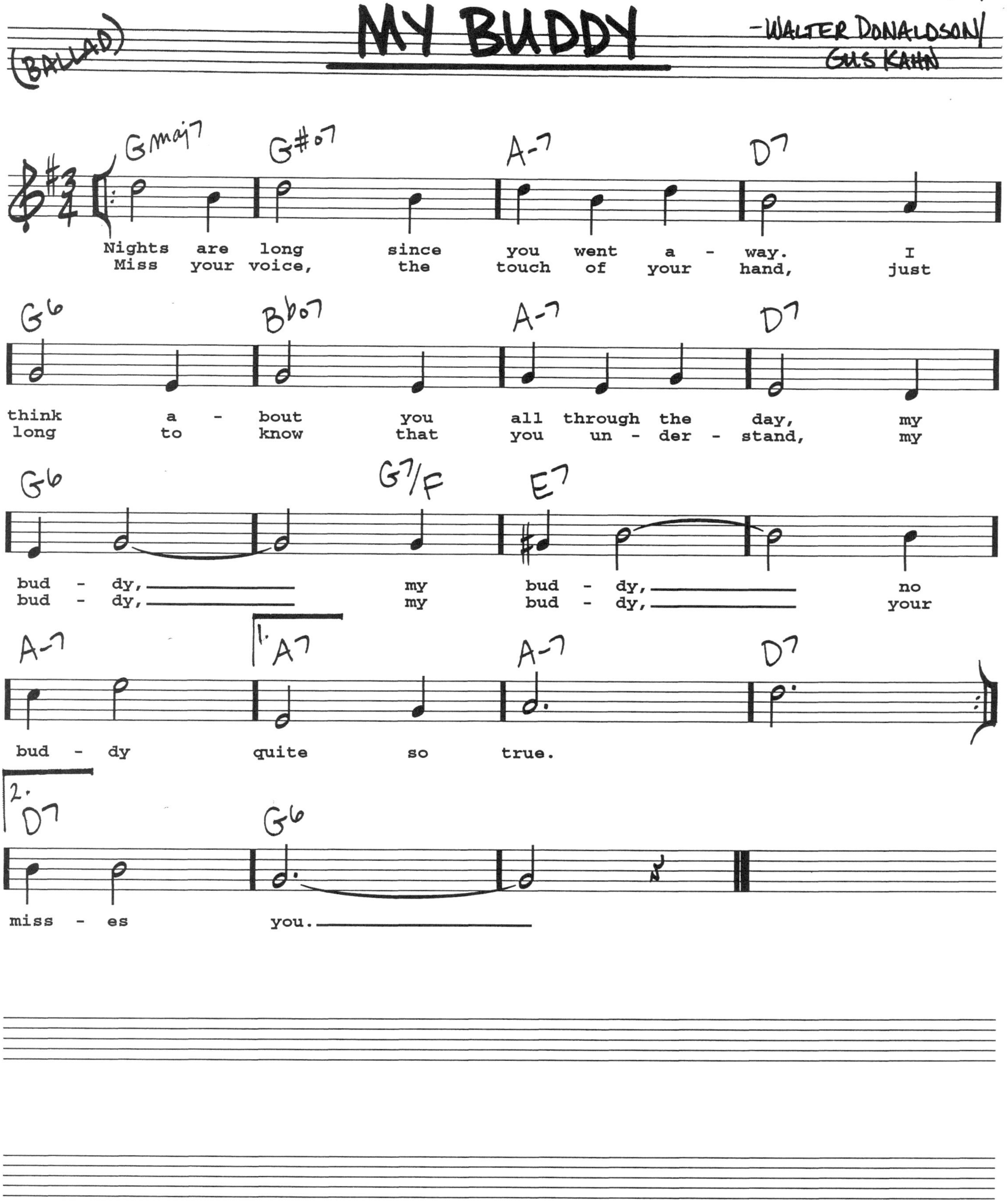

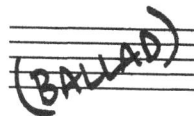

234

MY MELANCHOLY BABY

(MED.)

— Ernie Burnett / George A. Norton

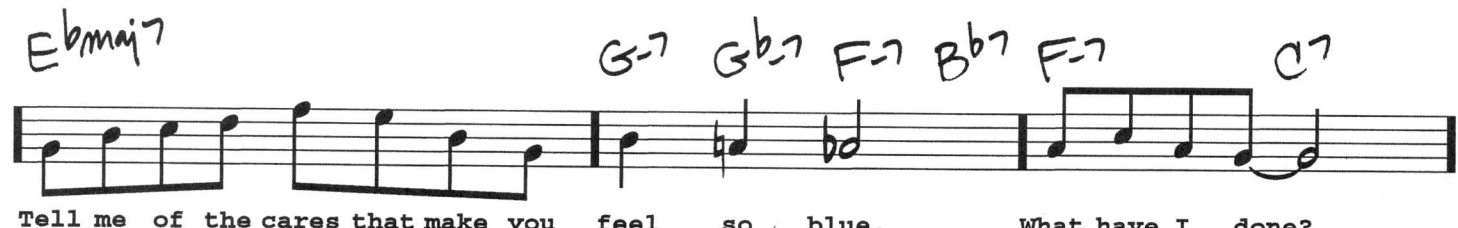

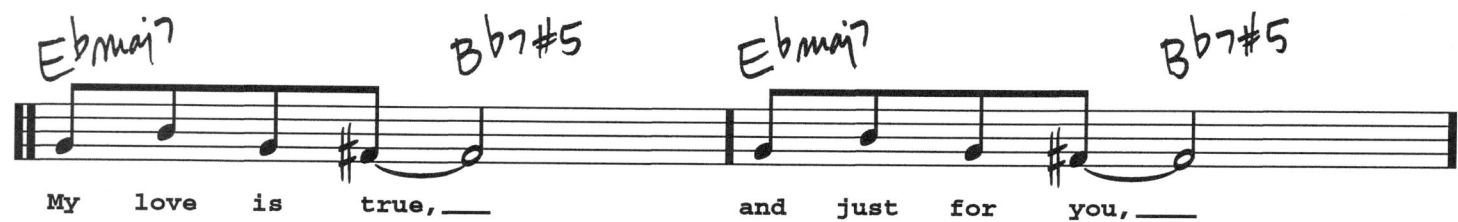

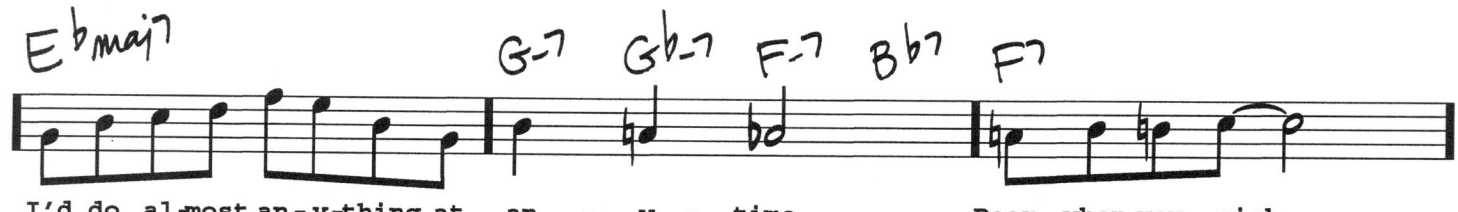

Copyright © 2007 by HAL LEONARD CORPORATION

(MED.)

MY SILENT LOVE

–DANA SUESSE/
EDWARD HEYMAN

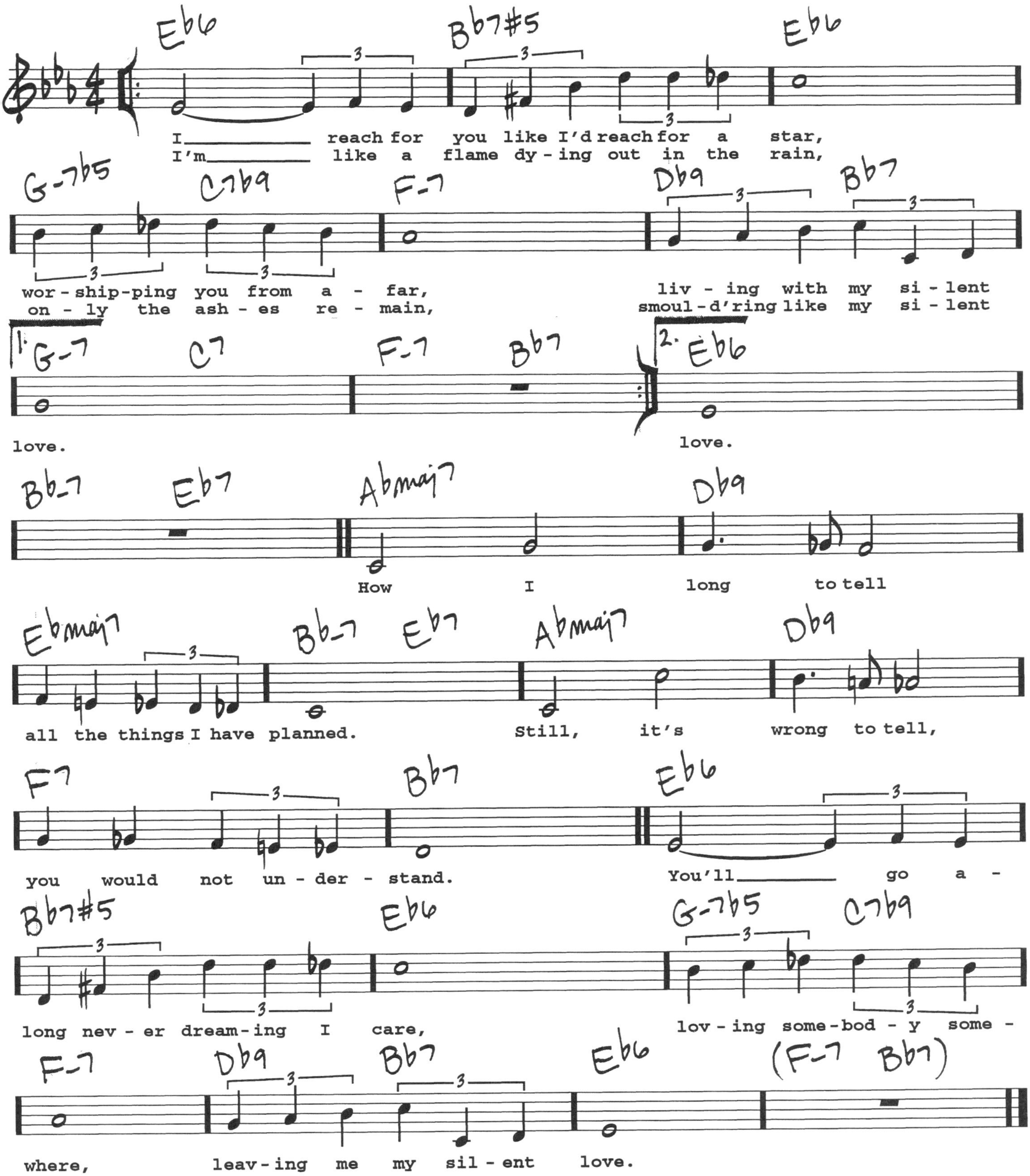

(MED. BALLAD)

MY SIN

–B.G. DeSYLVA/
LEW BROWN/
RAY HENDERSON

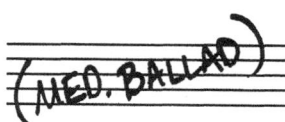

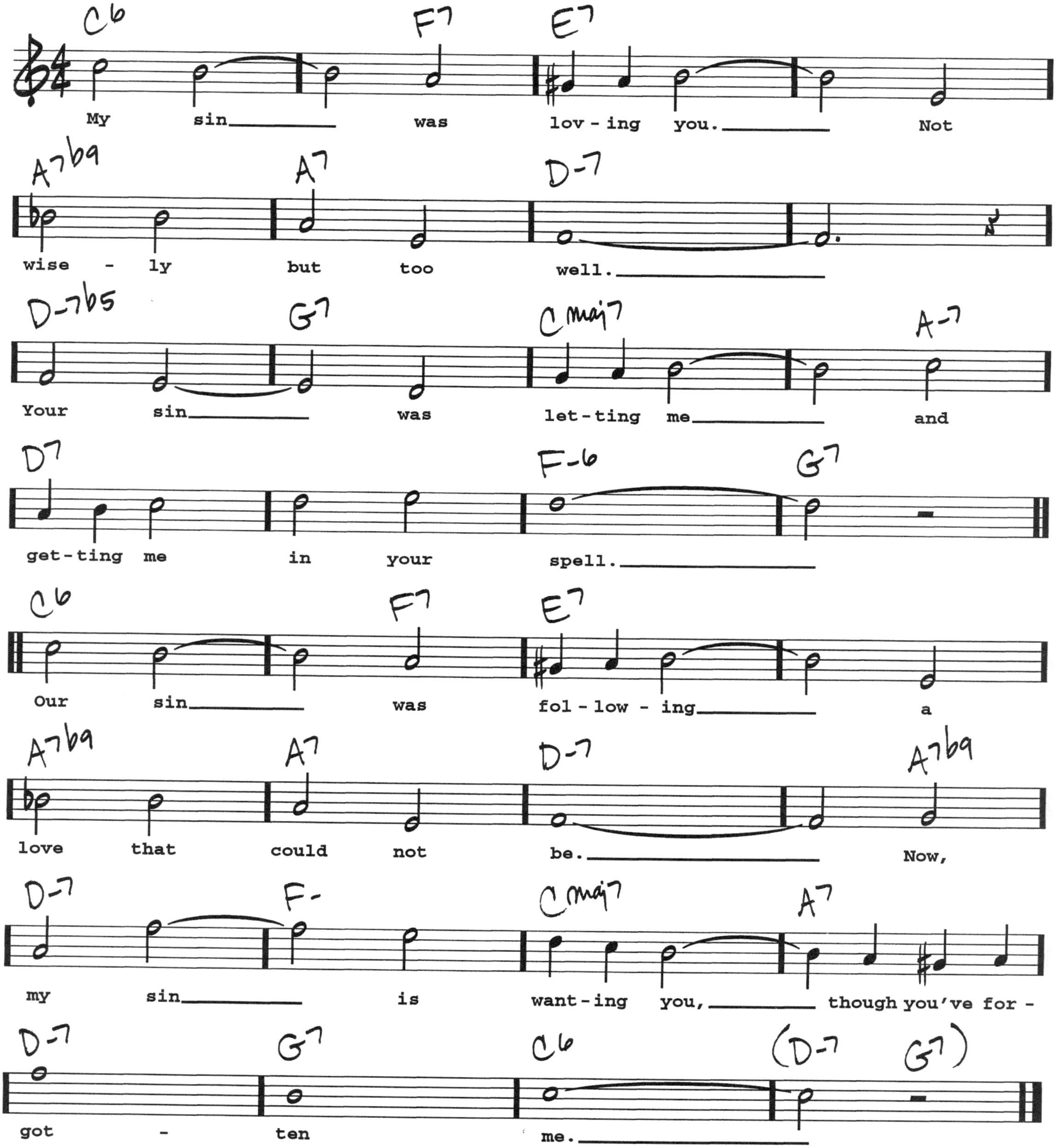

(MED. BALLAD)

NANCY – WITH THE LAUGHING FACE

– JAMES VAN HEUSEN / PHIL SILVERS

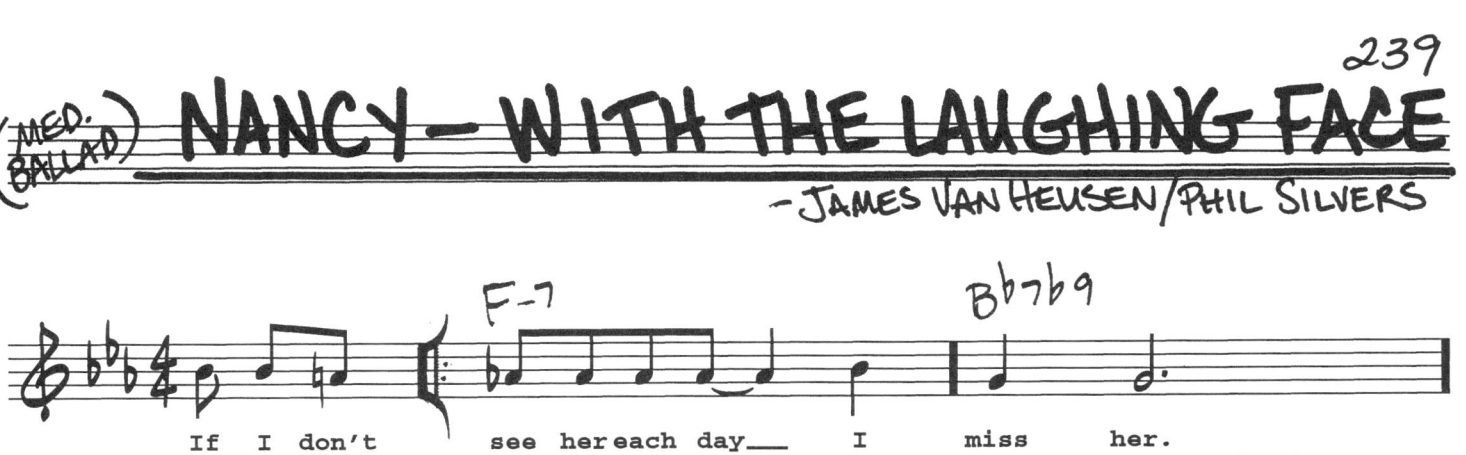

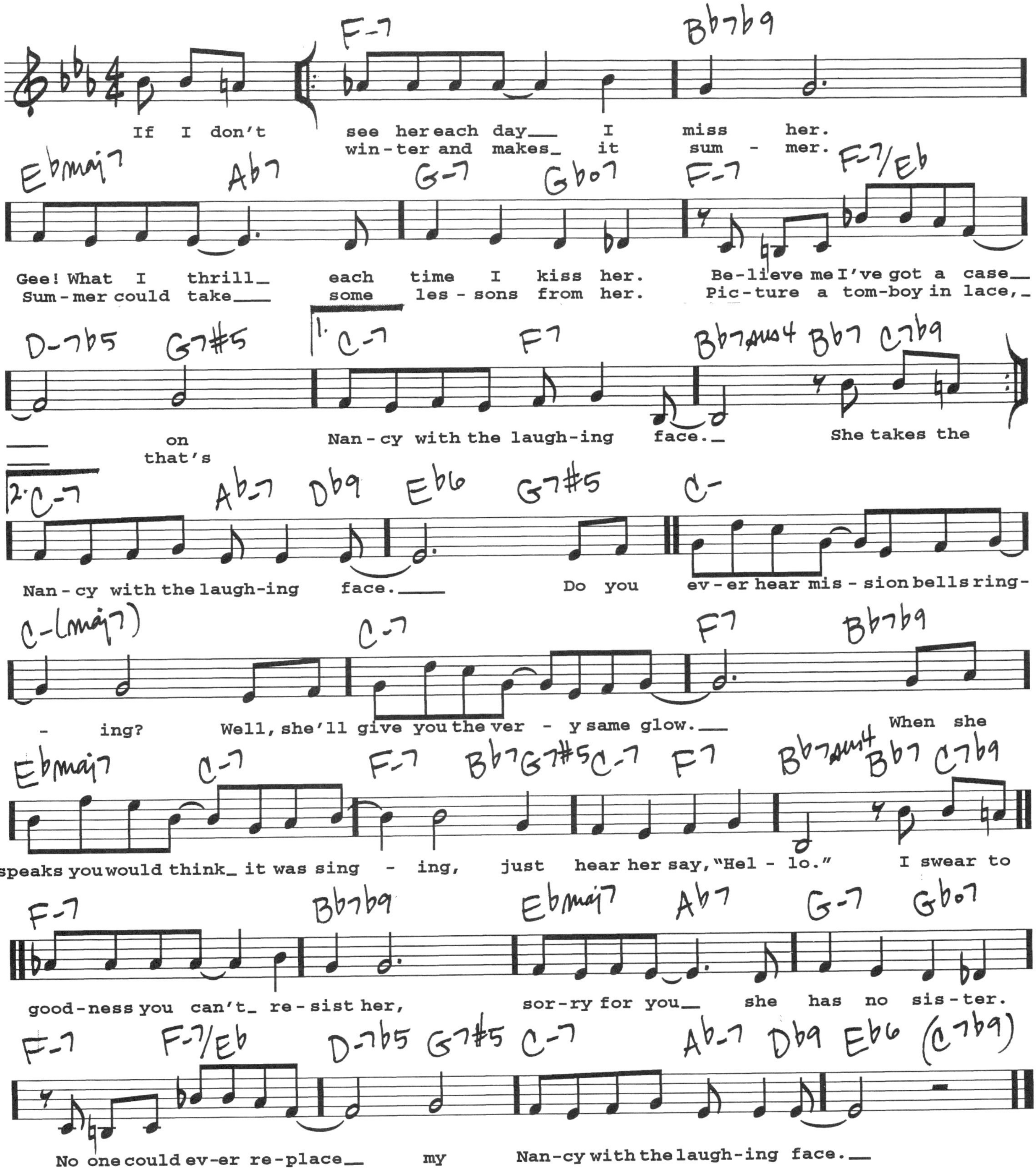

A Nightingale Sang In Berkeley Square

Manning Sherwin / Eric Maschwitz

That certain night, the night we met, there was magic abroad in the air. There were angels dining at the Ritz, and a nightingale sang in Berk-'ley Square.

may be right, I may be wrong, but I'm perfectly willing to swear that when you turn'd and smiled at me a

I

The moon that lingered over London town, poor puzzled moon, he wore a frown. How could he know we two were so in love? The whole damn world seemed upside down. The streets of town were paved with stars; it was such a romantic affair. And as we kiss'd and said "good-night," a nightingale sang in Berk-'ley Square.

Copyright © 1940 The Peter Maurice Music Co., Ltd., London, England
Copyright Renewed and Assigned to Shapiro, Bernstein & Co., Inc., New York for U.S.A. and Canada

NOBODY ELSE BUT ME

244
(MED. SWING)
— Jerome Kern / Oscar Hammerstein II

I want to be no one but me.

I am in love with a {lov-er / la-dy} who likes me the way I am.

I have my faults; {he / she} likes my faults.

I'm not ver-y bright; {he's / she's} not ver-y bright.

{He / She} thinks I'm grand; that's grand for me.

{He / She} may be wrong, but if we get a-long, what do we care, say we.

She: When he holds me close, close as we can be,
He: Walk-ing on the shore, swim-ming in the sea,

I tell the lad that I'm grate-ful and I'm glad that I'm
when I am with her I'm glad the boy who's with her is

no-bod-y else but me!
no-bod-y else but me!

Copyright © 1946 UNIVERSAL - POLYGRAM INTERNATIONAL PUBLISHING, INC.
Copyright Renewed

Peel Me A Grape
— Dave Frishberg

(Med. Slow)

Peel me a grape, crush me some ice. Skin me a peach, save the
Pop me a cork, french me a fry. Crack me a nut, bring a

fuzz for my pil-low. Start me a smoke, talk to me nice.
bowl full-a bon-bons. Chill me some wine, keep stand-in' by.

You got-ta wine me and dine me. Don't try and fool me,
Just en-ter-tain me, cham-pagne me. Show me you love me,

be-jewel me. Ei-ther a-muse me or lose me.
kid glove me. Best way to cheer me, cash-mere me.

I'm get-tin' hun-gry. Peel me a grape.

Here's how to be an a-gree-a-ble chap:

Love me and leave me in lux-u-ry's lap. Hop when I hol-ler,

skip when I snap. When I say, "Do it," jump to it.

© 1962 (Renewed) Swiftwater Music

PEOPLE

(BALLAD)

-JULE STYNE/ BOB MERRILL

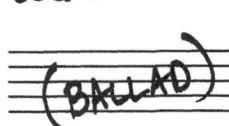

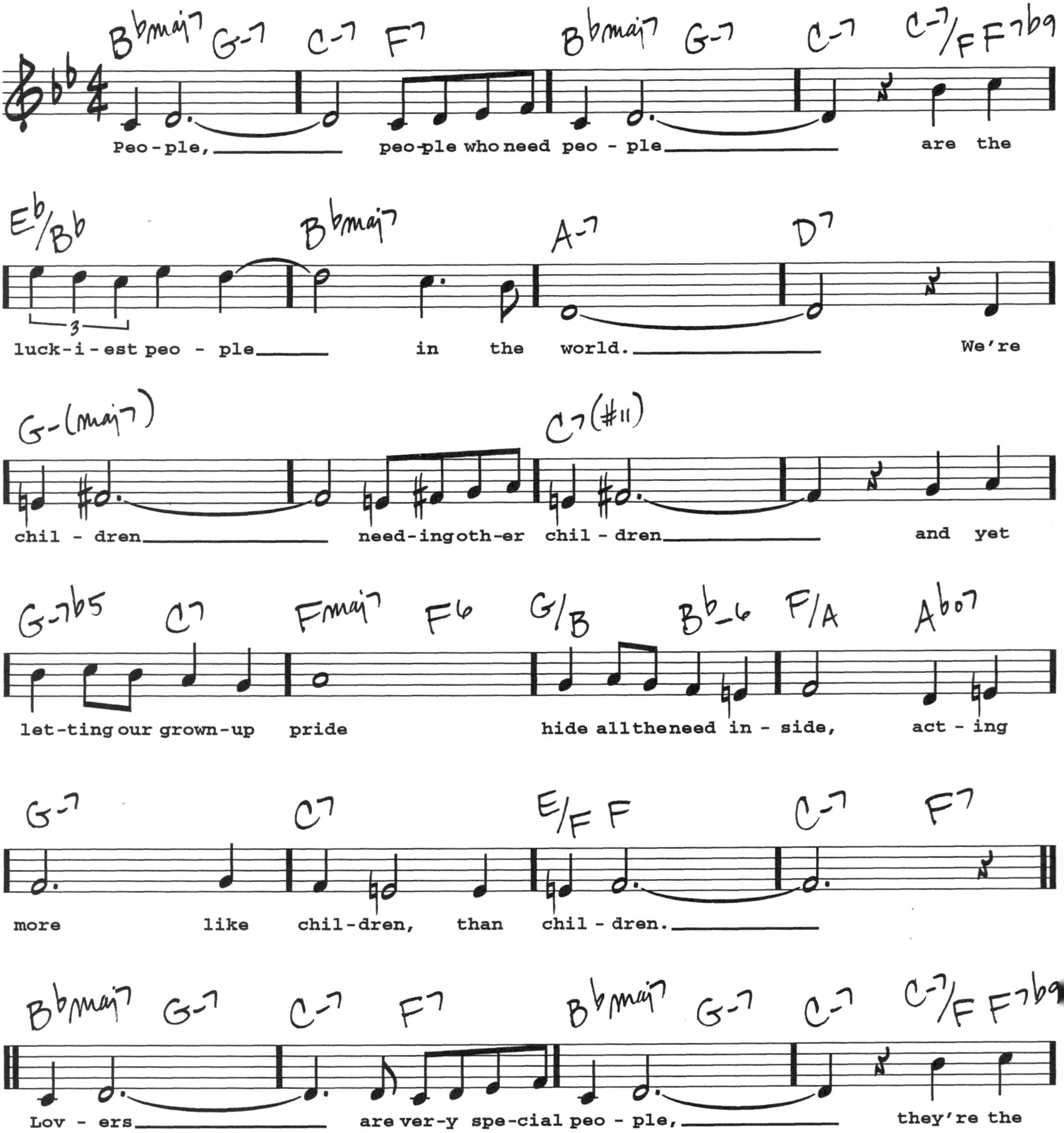

(BALLAD)

PRETEND

–LEW DOUGLAS/
CLIFF PARMAN/
FRANK LAVERE

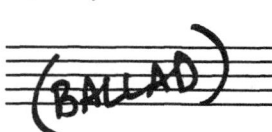

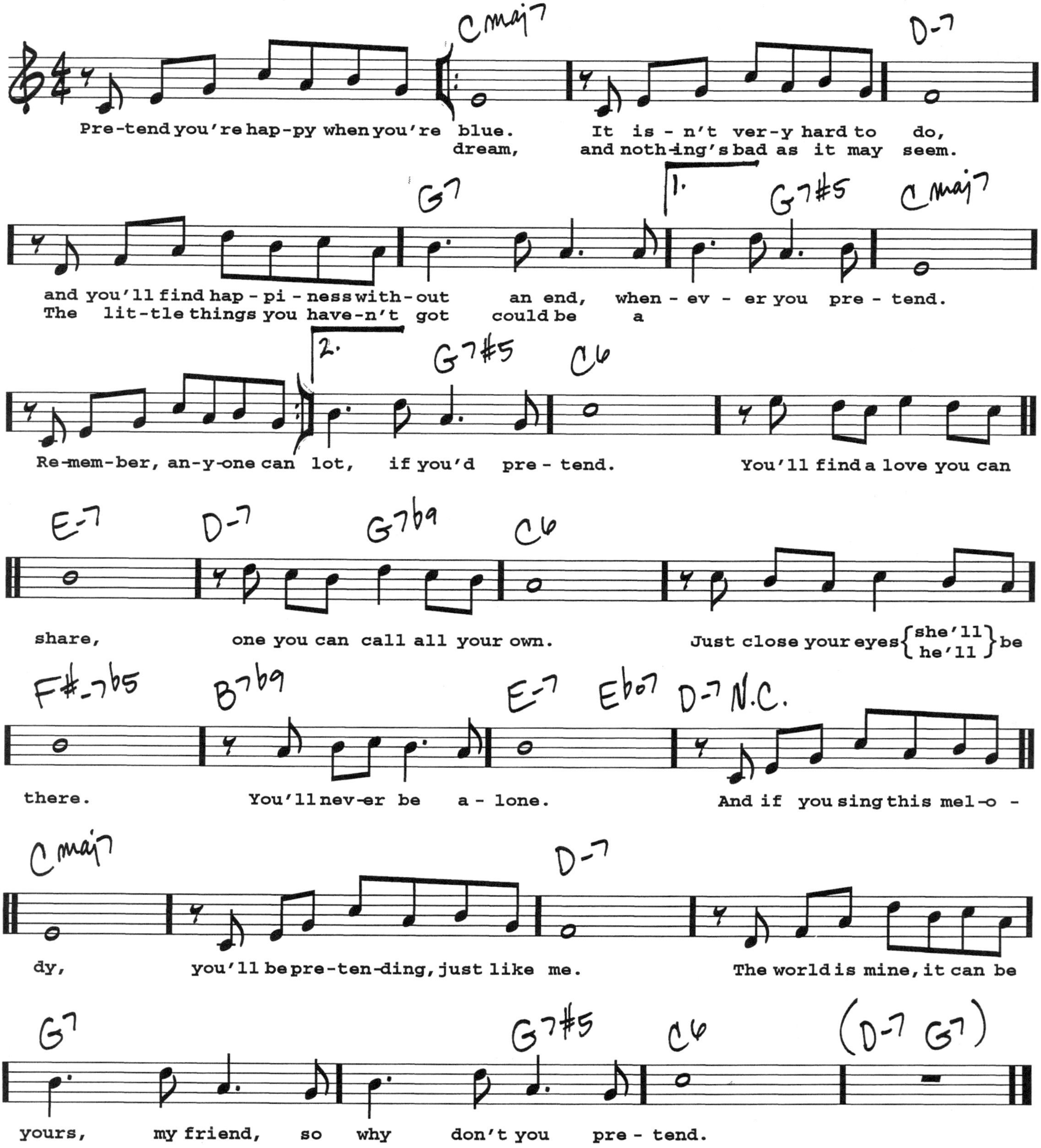

Additional Lyrics

Who said that every wish would be heard and answered
When wished on the morning star?
Somebody thought of that, and someone believed it;
Look what it's done so far.
What's so amazing that keeps us stargazing,
And what do we think we might see?
Someday we'll find it, the rainbow connection;
The lovers, the dreamers and me.

Have you been half asleep, and have you heard voices?
I've heard them calling my name.
Is this the sweet sound that calls the young sailors?
The voice might be one and the same.
I've heard it too many times to ignore it
It's something that I'm s'posed to be.
Someday we'll find it, the rainbow connection;
The lovers, the dreamers and me.

© 1979 Fuzzy Muppet Songs

Spanish Lyrics

Siempre que te pregunto
Que cuando como y donde, tu siempre nie respondes
Quizás, quizás, quizás.
Y así pason los días
Y yo desesperado y tú, tú contestando
Quizás, quizás, quizás.
Estás perdiendo el tiempo pensando, pensando;
Por lo que mas tu quieras hasta cuando, hasta cuando.
Yasí pasan los días
Y yo desesperado y tú, tú contestando
Quizás, quizás, quizás.

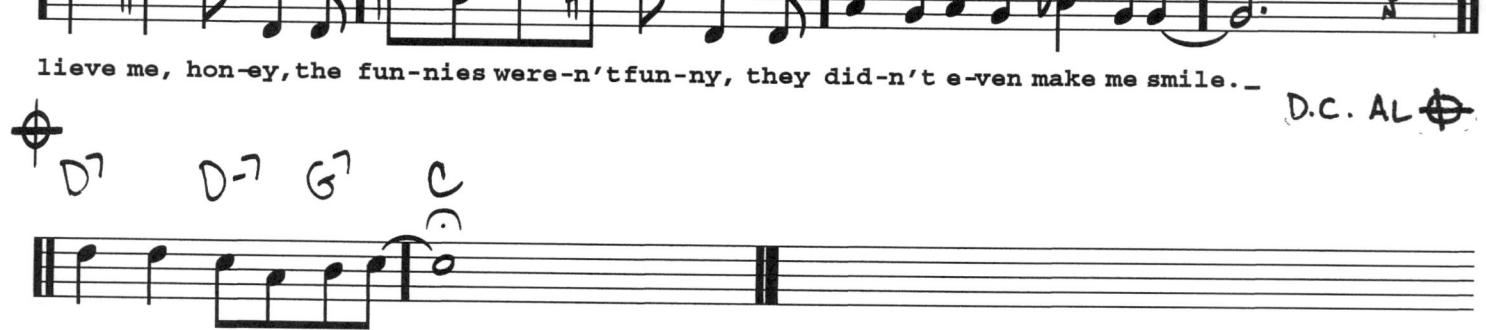

SKYLARK

(BALLAD)

- HOAGY CARMICHAEL/
JOHNNY MERCER

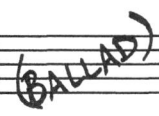

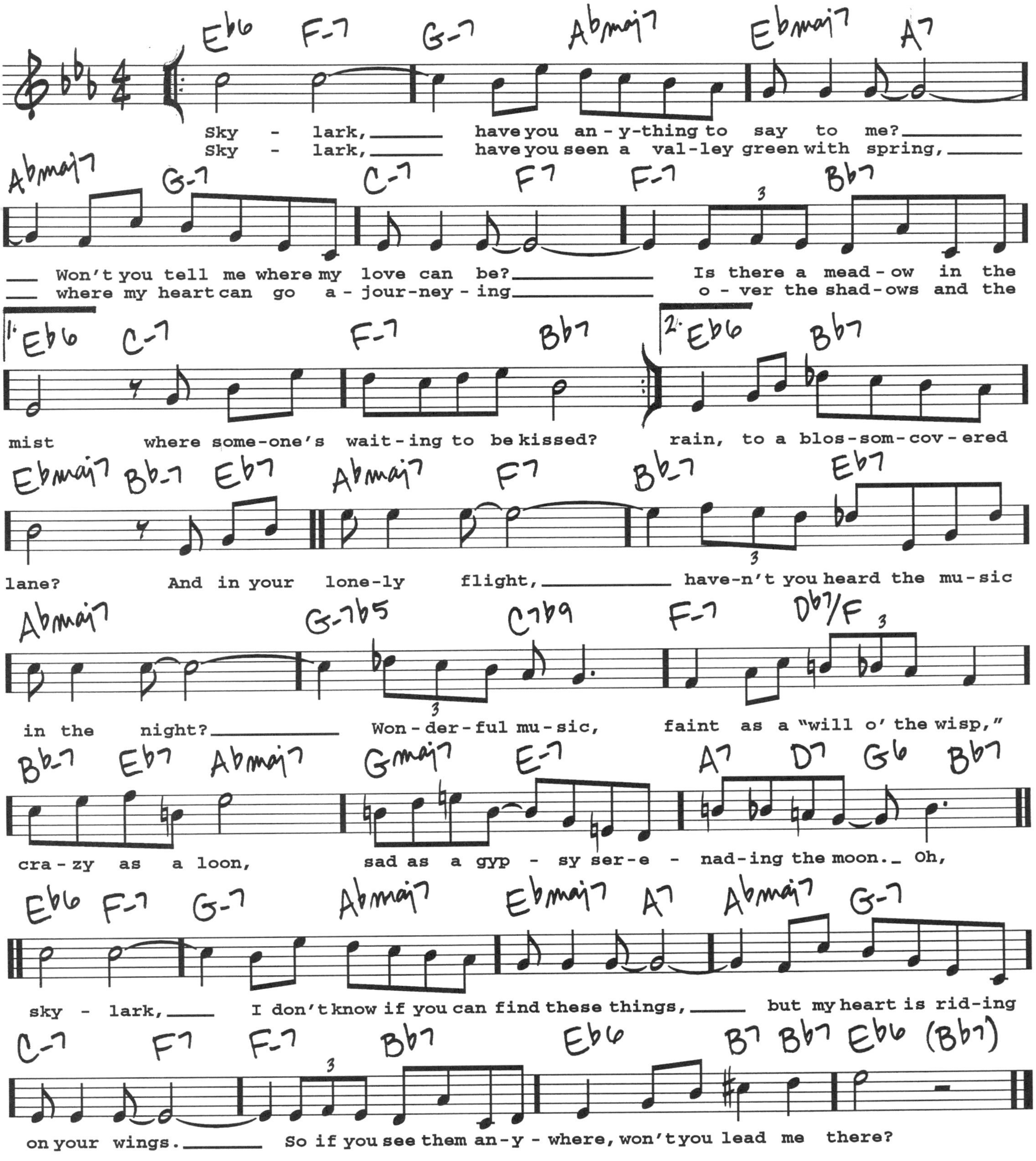

Spring Can Really Hang You Up The Most

302
(Ballad)
— Tommy Wolf / Fran Landesman

INTRO

Cmaj7 Bb7 Cmaj7 Bb7 Cmaj7

Once I was a sen-ti-men-tal thing, threw my heart a-way each spring.

Bb-7 Eb7sus4 Abmaj7 F#-7 B7sus4 Emaj7 D-7 G7sus4 Cmaj7 A-7

Now a spring ro-mance has-n't got a chance. Prom-ised my first dance to win-ter,

D-7 G7 E7#5 A7b9 D-7 A7b9 D7 G7

all I've got to show's a splin-ter for my lit-tle fling!

HEAD

Cmaj7 Bbmaj7 Cmaj7 Bbmaj7 Cmaj7 A-7 D-7 G7

Spring this year has got me feel-ing like a horse that nev-er left the
Morn-ing's kiss wakes trees and flow-ers, and to them I'd like to drink a

E-7 A7 F#-7b5 F-6 E-7 A-7 D7

post. I lie in my room, star-ing up at the ceil-ing.
toast. I walk in the park just to kill lone-ly hours.

1. D-7 G7 Cmaj7   2. D-7 G7 Cmaj7

Spring can real-ly hang you up the most!   Spring can real-ly hang you up the most!

G-7 Cmaj7 G-7 Cmaj7 G-7 Cmaj7

All af-ter-noon those birds twit-ter twit, I know the tune: "This is

G-7 Cmaj7 C-7 Fmaj7 C-7 Fmaj7

love, this is it!" Heard it be-fore and I know the score,

Additional Lyrics

Spring is here, there's no mistaking, robins building nests from coast to coast.
My heart tries to sing so they won't hear it breaking.
Spring can really hang you up the most!
College boys are writing sonnets, in the "tender passion" they've engrossed.
But I'm on the shelf with last year's Easter bonnets.
Spring can really hang you up the most!
Love came my way, I hoped it would last, we had our day, now it's all in the past.
Spring came along, a season of song full of sweet promise, but something went wrong!
Doctors once prescribed a tonic: "sulphur and molasses" was the dose.
Didn't help a bit, my condition…(To ⊕)

Spring Will Be A Little Late This Year

(Ballad) — Frank Loesser

304

© 1943 (Renewed) FRANK MUSIC CORP.

That's Life

Dean Kay / Kelly Gordon

(Slow Blues)

That's life, that's what people say. You're ridin' high in April, shot down in May. But I know I'm gonna change that tune, when I'm back on top in June. That's life, funny as it seems. Some people get their kicks steppin' on dreams. But I don't let it get me down, 'cause this ol' world keeps goin' around.

I've been a puppet, a pauper, a pirate, a poet, a pawn and a king. I've been up and down and over and out and I know one thing: each time I find myself flat on my face, I pick myself up and get back in the race.

That's life, I can't deny it, I thought of quitting, but my heart just won't buy it. If I didn't think it worth a try, I'd roll myself up in a big ball and die.

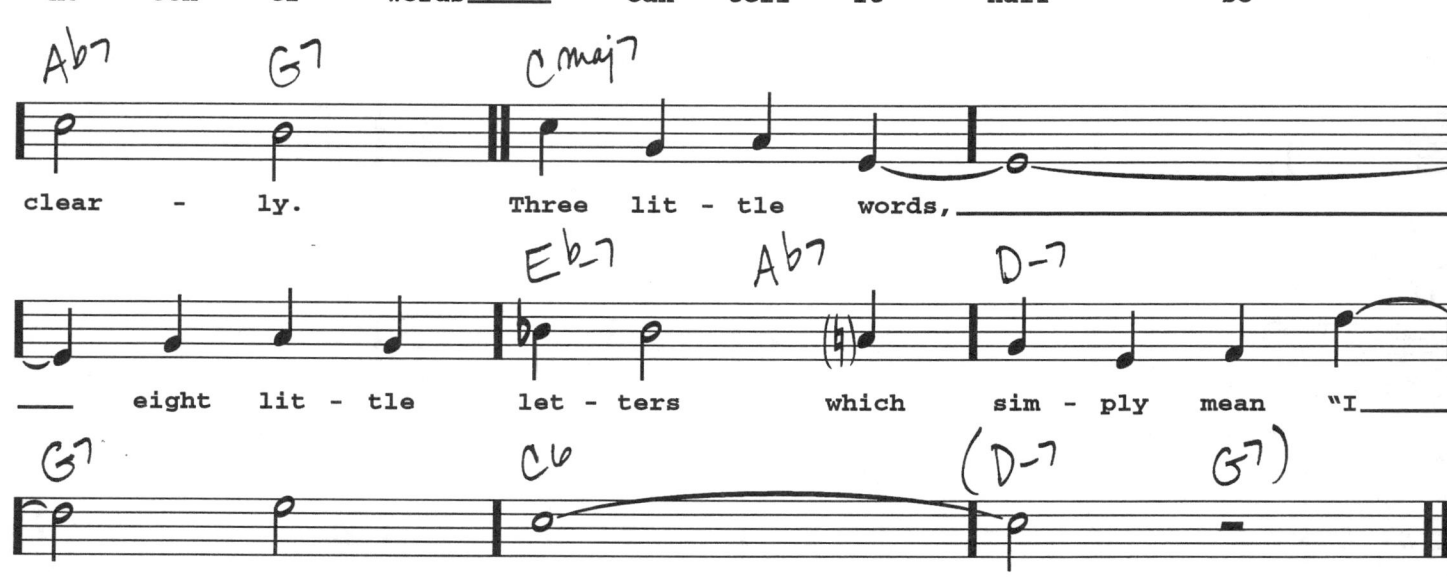

The Touch Of Your Lips

Med. Swing
— Ray Noble

337

The touch of your lips / touch of your hands upon my brow, / upon my head, your / the lips that are cool / love in your eyes and sweet; / a-shine; such / and tenderness lies in their soft caress, my heart forgets to beat. The now at last the moment divine, the touch of your lips on mine.

Copyright © 1936 by Chappell & Co.
Copyright renewed; extended term of Copyright deriving from Ray Noble assigned and effective February 26, 1992 to Range Road Music Inc. and Quartet Music

The Very Thought of You
— Ray Noble

(Ballad) 340

The ver-y thought of you, and I for-get to do the lit-tle or-di-nar-y things that ev-'ry-one ought to do. I'm liv-ing in a kind of day-dream, I'm hap-py as a king, and foolish tho' it may seem, to me that's ev-'ry- thing. The mere i- dea of you, the long-ing here for you, you'll nev-er know how slow the mo-ments go 'til I'm near to you. I see your face in ev-'ry flow-er; your eyes in stars a-bove. It's just the thought of you, the ver-y thought of you, my love.

MED. LATIN

WHAT A DIFF'RENCE A DAY MADE

– MARIA GREVER / STANLEY ADAMS

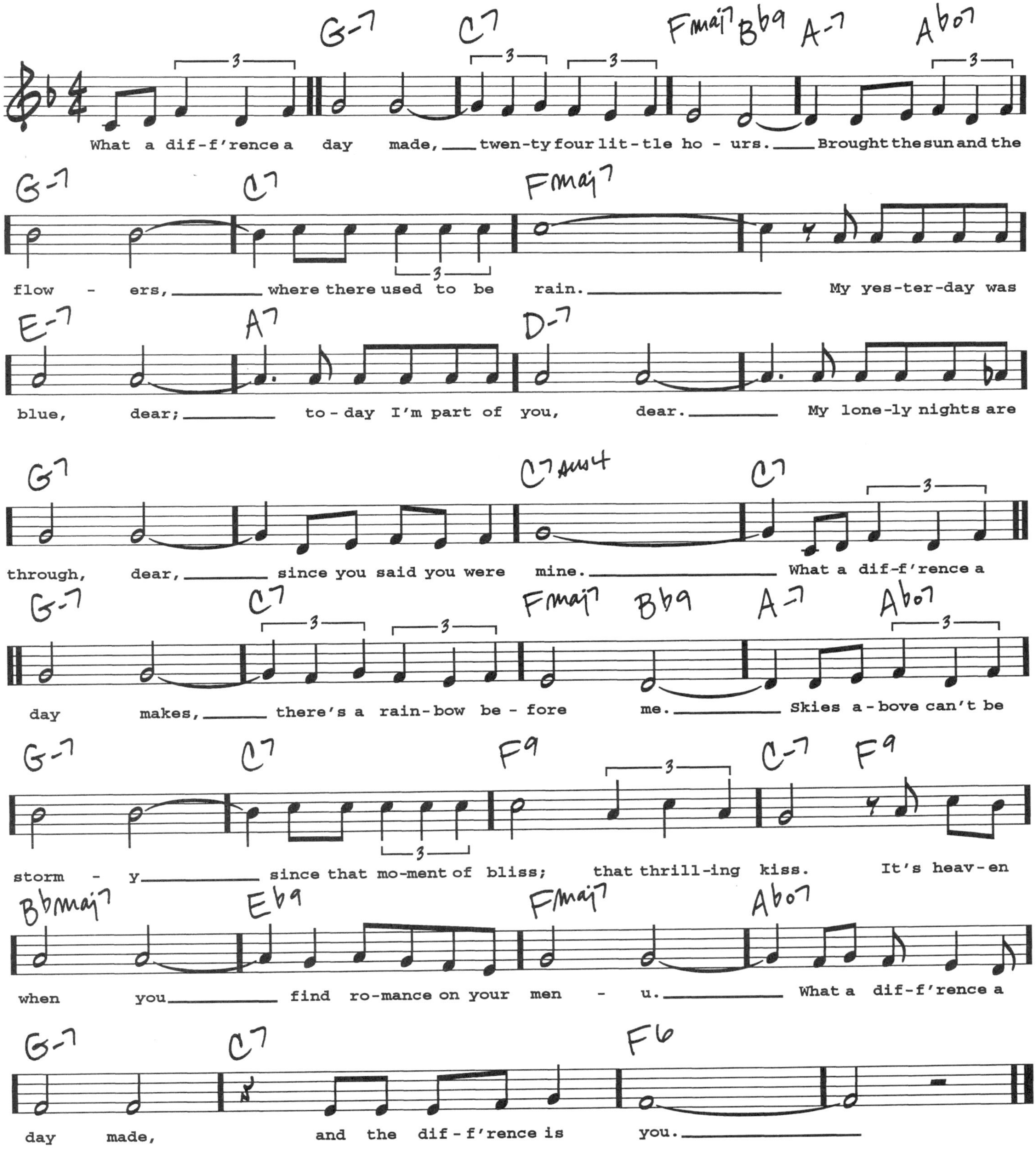

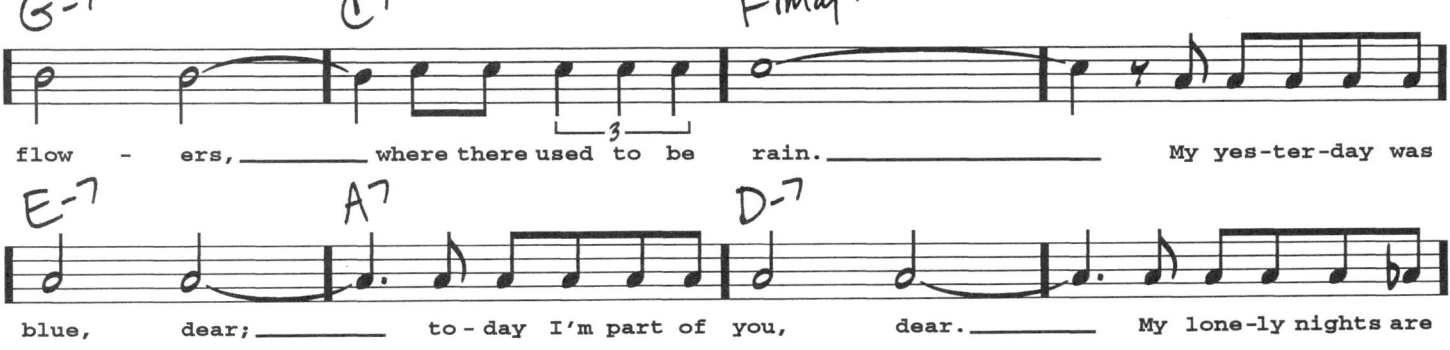

WHAT I DID FOR LOVE

(MED.)

-MARVIN HAMLISCH
EDWARD KLEBAN

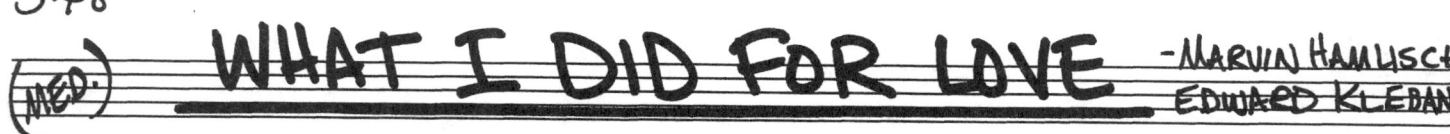

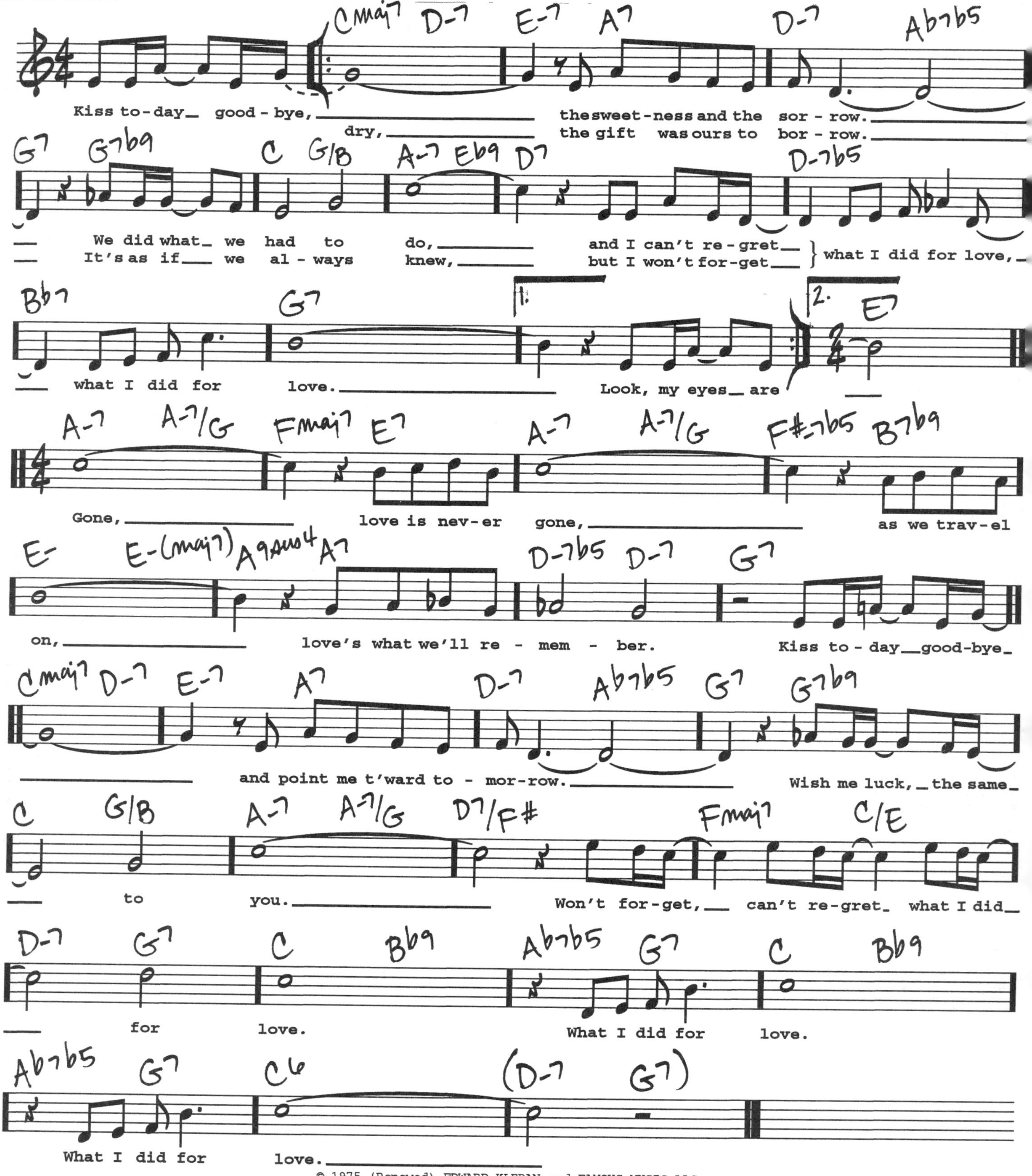

352
WHY DON'T YOU DO RIGHT
(GET ME SOME MONEY, TOO!)
—Joe McCoy

(MED. SWING)

You had plen-ty mon-ey nine-teen twen-'y two,— you let oth-er peo-ple make a fool of you.— Why don't you do right,_____ like some oth-er men do?_____ Get out of here and get me some mon - ey too._____ Yo' sit-tin' down_ won-d'ring what it's all a-bout,_ if you ain't got no mon-ey they will put you out._ Why don't you do right,_____ like some oth-er men do?_____ Get out of here and

© 1941, 1942 EDWIN H. MORRIS & COMPANY, A Division of MPL Music Publishing, Inc.
© Renewed 1969, 1970 MORLEY MUSIC CO.

360 YOU ARE BEAUTIFUL

(Med. Ballad)

— Richard Rodgers / Oscar Hammerstein II

You are beautiful, small and shy.
This I know of you, nothing more,

You are the girl whose eyes met mine just as your boat sailed by.
you are the girl whose eyes met mine

passing the river shore. You are the girl whose laugh I heard,

silver and soft and bright; soft as the fall of lo-tus leaves

brushing the air of night. While your flower boat

sailed away, gently your eyes looked back on mine.

Clearly you heard me say: "You are the girl I will love some

day."

Copyright © 1958 by Richard Rodgers and Oscar Hammerstein II
Copyright Renewed
WILLIAMSON MUSIC owner of publication and allied rights throughout the world

Spanish Lyrics
*Solamente una vez, amé en la vida,
solamente una vez, y nada más.
Una vez nada más en mi huerto brilló la esperanza,
la esperanza que alumbra el camino de mi soledad.
Una vez nada más se entrega el alma, con la dulce y total renunciación.
Y cuando ese milagro realiza el prodigio de amarse,
Hay campanas de fiesta que cantan en el corazón.*

You Better Go Now

Robert Graham / Bickley Reichner

(Ballad)

362

You bet-ter go now, be-cause I like you much too much; you have a way with you. You ought to know now, just why I like you ver-y much. The night was gay with you. There's the moon a-bove and it gives my heart a lot of swing. In your eyes there's love, and the way I feel it must be spring. I want you so now, you have the lips I love to touch; you bet-ter go now, you bet-ter go, be-cause I like you much too much.

Copyright © 1936 by Chappell & Co.
Copyright Renewed

REAL BOOKS AVAILABLE

C, B♭, E♭ & Bass Clef Editions for:

The Real Book – Sixth Edition, Volume 1

The Real Book – Second Edition, Volume 2

The Real Book – Second Edition, Volume 3

The Real Vocal Book – Volume 1

The Real Vocal Book – Volume 2

More editions coming soon.

See your music dealer to order.

7777 W. BLUEMOUND RD. P.O. BOX 13819 MILWAUKEE, WI 53213

Visit Hal Leonard Online at
www.halleonard.com